# Praise for *Becoming a Self-Reliant Leader*

"At Patagonia, our onsite childcare centers prize two qualities in our children: self-reliance and the ability to play well with others. These turn out to be our favorite attributes in employees as well. *Becoming a Self-Reliant Leadership* collects and distills the wisdom gained from these wilderness journeys, providing the solidly grounded, humble advice necessary for developing the ordinary daily courage it takes to do things right."

**—Vincent Stanley, Director of Philosophy, Patagonia, and Coauthor, *The Future of the Responsible Company***

"Jacquie Jordan has partnered with Jan Rutherford to explain, whether it is in the military or in business, how true leaders develop teams and themselves. Jacquie and Jan have created this book that will help leaders and teams as they face the difficulties and complexity of the modern world. This book should be read by all leaders looking to accomplish the impossible!"

**—Marene Allison, President, West Point Women, Class of 1980 West Point and Distinguished Graduate Award Recipient**

"*Becoming a Self-Reliant Leader* brings to light the raw, unvarnished truth about leadership. The book acts as a compass, guiding the reader to understand that the real transformation begins where comfort zones end. It's a must-read for those ready to face their own crucibles and lead with conviction and clarity."

**—Gino Wickman, Author, *Traction* and *Shine*, and Creator of EOS**

"Rutherford and Jordan are not only leaders but sages, and this book is a must-read modern classic. The book's chapters pace us through real-life parables that ooze wisdom about business and life. They are two of those rare teachers that unmask wisdom in such a way that you immediately recognize the applicability. This is a life changing tome."

**—Steve House, retired Professional Climber and Founder & CEO, Uphill Athlete**

"In any kind of extreme environment, survival is a team effort. Being part of a team I can count on is always critical to success when it comes to climbing big mountains—whether they are literal or figurative. The stories in this book capture the struggles of taking on the unknown and growing stronger in doing so, while bringing the lessons back to the office. You will laugh, be inspired, and become even more self-reliant."

**—Alison Levine, Adventurer and *New York Times* Bestselling Author, *On the Edge***

"*Becoming a Self-Reliant Leader* is not a precious gem—it's the diamond mine. It is that rare find that actually does more than challenge us to build our own narrative—it shows us the way. This book is a reference guide on how to become a transformational human being."

**—Tim Cole, Founder, The Compass Alliance**

"Jan and Jacquie have captured the essence of modern leadership in *Becoming a Self-Reliant Leader*. Their principles are how I tried to model my own leadership style while commander of the International Space Station."

**—Colonel Terry Virts, USAF (Ret.), former NASA astronaut and ISS Commander**

"*Becoming a Self-Reliant Leader* is a first-rate guide to building unstoppable teams not through the force of command and control but through the elegance of values and purpose. This book will help any group find their rhythm and thrive together."

**—Daniel H. Pink, #1 *New York Times* Bestselling Author, *The Power of Regret*, *When*, and *To Sell Is Human***

"Jan Rutherford and Jacquie Jordan have captured the very essence of leadership development. Using Rutherford's Crucible Expedition experiences, they capture leadership lessons as they emerge and are refined. This book is an exciting, entertaining, and insightful read, and you are guaranteed to capture numerous useful insights about how leadership develops and succeeds."

**—Kim Cameron, World-Renowned Scholar and Bestselling Author, *Positive Leadership***

"Managing others is a difficult process, but managing ourselves to do so properly can be just as challenging. Fortunately, this book gives us the tools to do both in a remarkably illuminating and engaging read."

**—Robert Cialdini, Author, *Influence* and *Pre-Suasion***

"Jan and Jacquie have just created the self-reliant leader's 'Swiss army leadership knife,' an essential requirement in every leader's rucksack. This book is a must for every leader's briefcase, rucksack, and bedside locker and every organization's essential reading list."

**—Vice Admiral (Rtd) Professor Mark Mellett DSM. Chief of Staff of Ireland's Defence Forces from September 2015 until September 2021**

"If you care about becoming a better leader, empowering your team, and leading your organization to reach new levels of performance and success, *Becoming a Self-Reliant Leader* is a must-read. Distilled from the authors' years of military experience, executive coaching, and leading crucible expeditions in the wilderness, this book offers invaluable guideposts on the journey to becoming the best leader you can be."

**—Michele Flournoy, Cofounder, WestExec Advisors, and former Undersecretary of Defense for Policy**

"Jan and Jacquie have written a book that is so insightful that I'm compelled to share it with my son, who is a budding Army leader. They seamlessly overlay Crucible Expedition experiences with commonly encountered leadership challenges in a way that is immediately valuable and applicable to your next venture or adventure. This book will make you a better leader, no matter where you are along the journey."

**—Millard View, CSM (Ret.), US Army Special Forces**

"Like the authors of *Becoming a Self-Reliant Leader*, I've led more than 200 international expeditions, using the mountains to teach leadership. As you'll learn in this book, these journeys are only nominally about the summit; rather, they are about the grit and discipline needed to forge teams. Any leader looking to test their mettle and truly understand the gravity of their decisions should consider this book their field guide to the heights of authentic leadership."

**—Chris Warner, CEO, Author, Leadership Educator, and the 2nd American to climb the world's fourteen highest peaks (the 8000 meter peaks)**

"*Becoming a Self-Reliant Leader* is the perfect blend of timeless wisdom and valiant approaches to leading through complexity. Rather than focusing solely on outward strategies for success, it encourages self-awareness as a foundational pillar of effective leadership. By mastering ourselves, we can better navigate the complexities of leading others."

**—Erin Shrimpton, Chartered Organizational Psychologist, LinkedIn Learning Instructor, Coach, and Consultant**

"Reading this book, I have the benefit of being poured into and leveraging the wisdom gained from the Crucible® experiences of Jan Rutherford and Jacquie Jordan and learning what it truly means to be a self-reliant leader, challenged on how to lead oneself and lead others."

**—Joseph D. Kenner, President & CEO, Greyston**

"Having participated in three Crucible Expeditions, I can personally validate the transformative journey leaders undertake when they're stripped of their titles and faced with nature's raw challenges. I believe any reader of this narrative will gain authentic and powerful insights that are as real as the triumphs and tribulations the book portrays."

**—Willis Wiedel, Founding Partner & CEO, Encore Electric, Inc.**

"Through years of leading high-performing teams, I've found that by creating a space for teammates to be deeply heard, they are more likely to align with the purpose of the organization while striving for continued growth for themselves and the team. This book gives leaders practical advice on how to create that culture—whether on the side of a mountain or in the office."

**—Tina Vatanka Murphy, President & CEO, Global Healthcare Exchange (GHX)**

"There are few people I would ever want to learn leadership from more than Jan Rutherford. The way he and his team have created crucibles that push leaders outside their comfort zone is so unique. This book takes you through what is required to become a self-reliant leader and I couldn't recommend it more highly."

**—Don Yaeger, 12x *New York Times* Bestselling Author**

"Today's leaders are hamstrung with so many definitions of what 'good' looks like, they are grasping at straws and getting little help. Our workplaces have been upended to an extensive degree, and what the 'new normal' will be has yet to be agreed upon. What's a leader to do? Fortunately, Rutherford and Jordan have dug deep and unearthed critical insights about how today's and tomorrow's leaders can thrive amid the process of becoming. If you're looking for a blueprint for shaping high-impact leadership for yourself and others, you're holding it."

**—Ron Carucci, Managing Partner, Navalent, and Bestselling and Award-winning Author, *Rising to Power* and *To Be Honest***

"*Becoming a Self-Reliant Leader* strikes a deep chord, reminding us that the essence of leadership is not found in titles but in trials. Jan Rutherford and Jacquie Jordan's book is a masterful blend of adventure, transformation, and leadership insights to help you forge a legacy of high trust and resilience."

**—Richie Norton, Bestselling Author, *Anti-Time Management***

"If you're looking for a kick in the pants (in book form!), you've found it. This book dives deep into what it means to lead yourself first, incorporating discipline, motivation, and strength. This is not a theory-based book; instead, it's packed with practical advice on how to cultivate these qualities in yourself and your team."

**—Kim Kaupe, Entrepreneur, Forbes 30 Under 30, Ad Age 40 Under 40, and *Inc.* magazine's 35 Under 35**

"The book captures the essence of transformative experiences that shape leaders in the face of adversity, mirroring the challenges we encounter in the ever-evolving landscape of healthcare. I see this book as an essential guide for any professional striving to navigate the complexities of leadership with a focus on a love of learning and the self-discipline of good old-fashioned hard work."

**—Michael Dowling, President and CEO, Northwell Health**

"There is something in this book for anyone intentionally cultivating their leadership capabilities regardless of how evolved they are. If you set a goal to read this book once a year and do the cultivation work between readings, you will find something new and even more powerful each time you read it!"

**—Lee Benson, CEO, Execute to Win / EXECUTE MasterMIND**

"Although few have answered the call to action to serve like Jan and Jacquie, all of us who desire to become the leader we imagine can benefit from their wisdom. If learning transformational insights that will help you take more control of your leadership story is important to you, apply fiercely everything they share in *Becoming a Self-Reliant Leader.*"

**—Bobby Herrera, Bestselling Author, *The Gift of Struggle*, and CEO, Populus Group**

"What makes *Becoming a Self-Reliant Leader* so compelling is Jan and Jacquie's unique ability to beautifully marry the challenges of trekking outdoors in the most extreme conditions and crystalizing its lessons into key leadership principles."

**—Jessica Chen, Emmy-Award Winner and Author, *Smart, Not Loud***

"*Becoming a Self-Reliant Leader* takes leadership learnings to the next level. The concepts of grit, ownership, and tribe are illustrated in real narrative examples that we find ourselves in every day, and it's not always pretty. This is not a book for the fainthearted, but those who wish to rise to the challenge of leadership at the highest level."

**—Kimberly Jung, CEO, Blanchard House, and Cofounder & former CEO, Rumi Spice, former Combat Army Engineer Platoon Leader**

"Jan and Jacquie's *Becoming a Self-Reliant Leader* brilliantly fuses military strategy with corporate wisdom to create a leadership guide that is both practical and profound. This book is an indispensable tool for leaders cultivating resilience and trust within their team."

**—Preston Pysh, Founder, Pylon Holding Company**

"As someone who has been fortunate enough to participate in a Crucible®, I can attest that the lessons learned out in the wilderness, as well as from the amazing men and women of our military who attended, translate directly to business."

**—Tom Pitstick, Chief Strategy Officer, Gates**

"In *Becoming a Self-Reliant Leader*, Jan and Jacquie masterfully intertwine the essence of leadership with the resilience of the human spirit. This book is a beacon for those aspiring to lead with purpose, demonstrating how the journey of self-reliance is both a personal commitment and a strategic advantage in the art of negotiation and beyond."

**—Kwame Christian, Esq., MA, CEO, The American Negotiation Institute, and Host of #1 Negotiation podcast, *Negotiate Anything***

"This book is a practical guide for how leaders can truly have an impact on their teams by leveling up their leadership skills. As a former Crucible® participant, I can tell you firsthand how impactful these leadership lessons have been for me, the teams I lead, and my organization."

**—Erin Procko, Twin Cities President, Bell Bank**

"Reading about others' experiences on expeditions brought great color to the leadership lessons in *Becoming a Self-Reliant Leader*. By owning your behaviors and allowing yourself to be vulnerable, you increase your team's trust in you. By building the 'right' versus the 'best' team, and demonstrating your belief in their ability, you build a high-performing team. I have leveraged the insights and seen results."

**—Kate Eary, General Counsel, Gentex Corporation**

"Finally, we have a fresh perspective on leadership development. *Becoming a Self-Reliant Leader* takes you on a journey of leadership by getting to the core of what separates the good from the great."

**—Sean Conley, Learning Executive and President, ConleyGlobal**

"Often, true leadership is about finding inside yourself the determination, creativity, and resilience needed to make tough decisions while nurturing truly exemplary teams. The Crucible® helps executives unlock these inner qualities to become visionary and inspirational leaders."

**—Ciaran Flanagan, Strategic Consultant, MD Idea, and Director, Biobank, Ireland**

"This book is a must-have resource for both leadership practitioners and scholars. It provides highly-relevant insights for leaders who are looking to enhance their ability to build adaptive teams in the context they serve. And, it provides a unique and enduring contribution to those who are passionate about intentionally developing leaders through challenging experiences and transformative reflection in the community."

**—Nate Allen, PhD, Colonel (Ret.) and President, TribusAllen**

# BECOMING A SELF-RELIANT LEADER

**Also by Jan Rutherford**

*The Littlest Green Beret: On Self-Reliant Leadership*

Coauthor of *Purposeful People: Business Leaders Making a Difference*

# BECOMING A SELF-RELIANT LEADER

## How Grit and Disciplined Duty Forge Indomitable Teams

**JAN RUTHERFORD and JACQUIE JORDAN**

MATT HOLT

Matt Holt Books
An Imprint of BenBella Books, Inc.
Dallas, TX

Matt Holt is an imprint of BenBella Books, Inc.
10440 N. Central Expressway
Suite 800
Dallas, TX 75231
benbellabooks.com
Send feedback to feedback@benbellabooks.com

*BenBella* and *Matt Holt* are federally registered trademarks.

Printed in the United States of America
10 9 8 7 6 5 4 3 2 1

Library of Congress Control Number: 2023059785
ISBN 9781637745595 (hardcover)
ISBN 9781637745601 (electronic)

Editing by Katie Dickman
Copyediting by Michael Fedison
Proofreading by Becky Maines and Marissa Wold Uhrina
Text design and composition by PerfecType, Nashville, TN
Cover design by Brigid Pearson
Cover photography by Jan Rutherford
Printed by Lake Book Manufacturing

*Honoring the men and women, executives and veterans, who embarked on our Crucible Expeditions, for their commitment to growth and paying forward the enduring lessons of grit and duty.*

*A portion of the proceeds from the sale of this book will be distributed to nonprofit organizations serving active-duty military and veterans.*

# CONTENTS

*Foreword by General Stanley A. McChrystal* xvii

*What Is a Self-Reliant Leader?* xxi

*Introduction* 1

**CHAPTER 1. SELECTION**

*Selecting the Right People vs. the Best People* 9

**CHAPTER 2. PREPARATION**

*Getting Squared Away* 31

**CHAPTER 3. FIRST ENCOUNTER**

*Being Authentic and Vulnerable* 51

**CHAPTER 4. MOVEMENT**

*Setting Direction, Pace, and Tone* 67

**CHAPTER 5. BASE CAMP**

*Reenergizing and Reengaging* 89

**CHAPTER 6. FIRESIDE CHAT**

*Accelerating Relationships* 109

**CHAPTER 7: WHO'S WHO?**

*Cultivating the Group Dynamic* 127

**CHAPTER 8: OBSTACLES**
*Expecting Adversity* 149

**CHAPTER 9: RHYTHM**
*Creating Synergy* 169

**CHAPTER 10: TRIBAL CONNECTIONS**
*Cementing Commitments* 193

**CHAPTER 11: THE CRUX**
*Bringing It All Together* 213

**CHAPTER 12: THE END IS ANOTHER BEGINNING**
*Paying It Forward* 231

*Conclusion* 243

*Crucible Testimonials* 251

*Notes* 255

*Acknowledgments* 259

# FOREWORD

*by General Stanley A. McChrystal*

There is a blue serenity around the Jefferson Memorial before the sun rises. I try to arrive before anyone else, to see the moonlight reflected on the tidal basin. After so many years of morning exercise, I have seen the monuments in every season, and with each, there is a different kind of exquisite tranquility. The autumn leaves fall silently, the frosty slickness of the winter's ground morphs into the brightness of spring colors, and the summer brings humidity so thick that the heat waves ripple off the blacktop.

The only thing better than a run along the monuments alone is the opportunity to share the experiences with others. After leaving the military, I wondered how the rituals of my daily life, like my jogs before dawn, would look from the eyes of a civilian. This question drove me to create a company that applies the lessons of the Joint Special Operations Command (JSOC) to Fortune 500 companies. In an effort to guide leaders from the private sector, I looked to my own combat experience to strike the right balance between hierarchical and decentralized teams, both in mindsets and in structures. One of my first choices, to the surprise of many of my colleagues, was to take our clients on a sunrise monument run before any business engagements.

I like to think we have it down to a science by now; my team arrives at 5 AM, each with an individual assignment, leading a group of (often) bewildered executives. We always begin with one of my colleagues offering an explanation of our purpose, particularly why the military values (and West Point mandates) physical training. I always stand back and listen, reminding myself of the unspoken reason that these morning adventures hold tremendous meaning for me. Leaders are not forged within their comfort zones; rather, leaders find their footing when they are challenged, particularly in new contexts.

On our monument runs, I have seen leaders across all sectors—bankers, technologists, academics, and more—struggle to find their footing. This is a new arena for many of these successful business trailblazers, given that they have not felt the pavement of Washington, D.C., change under their shoes each morning as I have. Some lag behind the rest while others lean on their colleagues to keep the pace more manageable. Likewise, I have seen young analysts bring new energy to the runs, asking tough questions about the monument's history and pairing up with leaders who aren't usually wearing running shorts and jogging next to them.

Across the board, one thing is constant—each person completes the exercise. We complete this run with our clients not to humble anyone or overwhelm them, but to remind every person of the importance of inner strength. By placing everyone at every level on the same playing field, they can all meet a unique challenge in their own ways and flex new leadership muscles that they didn't know they have. Everyone can take their own lessons from the experience, but I hope that they all leave with the belief that they can adapt to new challenges and thrive outside of their offices.

Few know the importance of leadership development more than Jan Rutherford and Jacquie Jordan. Both have made careers in teaching leaders that the only way to know their true ability is to push themselves to new limits. They do so through innovative and collaborative experiences—together, they have led missions, which they call "Crucibles," in every imaginable context, from the deserts of Moab to the Juneau Ice Cap. What I have observed in our early morning monument sprints is only a sliver of what Jan and Jacquie have been able to learn from these Crucibles. Together, they have brought fresh insight and unprecedented thoughtfulness to the meaning of leader expeditions.

By writing *Becoming a Self-Reliant Leader: How Grit and Disciplined Duty Forge Indomitable Teams*, Jan and Jacquie share the lessons they have learned in their travels. By providing both their own philosophical perspective and the voices of those who have made these treks, their book provides a window into leadership at every level. Most importantly, they have found a way to universalize the lessons of their book. While both authors have extensive experience in the armed forces context, they recognize that there is tremendous value in finding the intersection of business and military leadership. This is an uncommon and critically understudied space—I have sought to explain the civil–military connection for years, but Jan and Jacquie bring it to life with each chapter of this deep and thoughtful text. Each expedition pairs veterans with private sector executives, and together they navigate the wilderness with only each other and their true grit. This combination of skill sets is instructive for each participant, and now that they have compiled their joint ventures into a book, it can instruct us all.

Jan and Jacquie's work shows the kaleidoscopic nature of leadership—from every perspective, leaders face a challenge. It is critical for individuals to learn about leading themselves, leading others, and leading their organization. Those three complementary features are the core of successful, mature, and empathetic leadership, whether within the U.S. military, a Fortune 500 company, or in the depths of the Grand Canyon. Our ability to achieve our goal is a product of our ability to find our inner groundbreaker, to push past our limits, and to see the bigger picture, no matter where we are. With *Becoming a Self-Reliant Leader*, we have unfettered access to how to begin that process, and how to extend ourselves to new heights in our ethics, our capacity for courage, and our ability to remain resilient amid ever-growing uncertainty.

Our monument run ends at the Lincoln Memorial, where I ask everyone to face the Capitol, their own images shining back in the Reflecting Pool. One of my favorite facts about the site is that Lincoln continued the construction of the Capitol's dome despite its cost and distraction from the war effort. He wanted to make the point that the United States' future as a unified nation was not in doubt. I love that Jan and Jacquie take that lesson to a new stratosphere. The book you are about to read is a testament to the idea that leadership is not a checklist, but a practice. It is a continuous unmasking of ourselves, an assessment of our weaknesses, and a constant striving to come into our power. While leadership has no end, I have confidence that its beginning can be found in *Becoming a Self-Reliant Leader*: let Jan and Jacquie take you on an unforgettable adventure through its forthcoming pages. If you do, I am confident you'll come out the other side as I have—with a new perspective on nature's inevitable challenges, a new desire to find your own noble purpose, and a proud readiness to embark on your own crucible. If you ask me, you'll be better for having run the race.

# WHAT IS A SELF-RELIANT LEADER?

**They lead themselves.**

A self-reliant leader is *squared away*—they take **ownership** of being prepared, competent, confident, disciplined, fair, reliable, resilient, responsive, resourceful, curious, and authentic, and they act as a role model for virtue and **grit** (a combination of passion, determination, and persistence).

**They lead others.**

By example, they cultivate shared **ownership** and a sense of **duty** that builds trust and a common purpose for the team.

**They lead the organization.**

They're **focused** on what matters most, and they seek **alignment** throughout the organization. They always uphold the values and standards so people and teams thrive to produce superior outcomes through clear *direction*, a sustainable *pace*, and a *tone* that energizes.

# INTRODUCTION

> "What happens during the Crucible and what happens afterward are not independent things . . . what happens going forward matters just as much."
>
> —*Jim Peters, Executive Participant, Wallowa Mountains, Oregon*

They could feel the sun beating down on the back of their necks, sweat forming on their brows. Only nine in the morning and the temperature was already hitting the high eighties. A nervous excitement was palpable. The group, made up of business executives and entrepreneurs, chatted idly in their brand-new outdoor gear and barely worn hiking boots. This was a new experience for most of them, out from behind their desks and in an unfamiliar environment. They worked in tech, engineering, and insurance, all more used to sitting in meetings and staring at screens than trekking through narrow slot canyons.

As they came around the next bend, they were hit with a view of the vast desert opening up before them. Their chatter ceased, as they all stood there, realizing for the first time this was not the typical team-building, kumbaya retreat. What they didn't know yet was that in the coming days, they would be physically, mentally, and emotionally tested unlike ever before, and they would come out on the other side of this journey transformed.

Their crucible had begun.

A crucible is a ceramic container in which metals are melted so they can be forged into something stronger. It's also a severe test in which people can be shaped into something indomitable, a trial from which they emerge more durable and resourceful than ever imagined. Experiencing a crucible changes people's narratives, helping them learn about who they truly are and who they can become. Shaped by adversity and challenge, such a journey leads to insights, revelations, and lessons that help people understand how purpose and meaning are inextricably linked to the components of a "good life." More importantly, reflection on the experience helps answer the question, "For whose good do I serve?" And that answer is the foundation of what it means to live intentionally, purposefully, and successfully.

For many leaders today, though, success may be fleeting. You may personally feel at your wit's end, which is understandable, considering what you are up against: Team dysfunction. Stifling repetition. Unrealistic financial goals. Abounding uncertainties. A worldwide employee engagement level of only 23 percent.[1] Burnout and crisis fatigue are real threats, and the constant shuffling of piecemeal careers seems to be far from slowing down.[2] Maybe you feel like you just need to forge ahead with the same old same old, exerting your will, persuading, selling, cajoling, and marketing your "brand." But this antiquated approach will no longer work, if it ever truly did.

These contemporary challenges require you to become a true team player, one who knows how and when to lead, but also how and when to follow; when to take a step back, give up control, and let others work toward solutions. To do so, you need to recognize not just your own strengths and capabilities, but those of your team members. You must grow your organization by developing yourself and the people you lead, not through a yearning for power and position, but through the desire to see everyone involved realize their own aspirations. You cannot get there unless you first reflect on the changes required, throttle back on strengths that no longer serve you, and correct for shortcomings to push ahead. Only then can you effectively serve those whom you lead.

This personalized approach is the future of leadership, and it depends on a shared trust that is so strong it's palpable. To achieve this mutual trust, you have to place trust in others, provide them with autonomy, empower them, and believe in their ability to make the right decisions. Simply put, you need to give trust to get trust in return. In practice, that means relinquishing control and accepting the consequences of an empowered team.

Of course, this, too, is a challenge.

## THE CRUCIBLE® EXPEDITION

The Crucible Expedition is a multi-day wilderness retreat, in which everyday business leaders are paired with military veterans, pitting themselves against the elements and overcoming obstacles in remote locales. In the process, participants have revelations about their personal and professional lives that prove to be as applicable in the boardroom as they are in the wild. Through these experiences, leaders come to better understand themselves as individuals, teammates, and leaders, while discovering how to design and create an environment that fosters trust, accountability, alignment, and focus. These expeditions take courage, curiosity, and grit, all of which can be forged when people are a little stressed, stretched, tired, and uncomfortable.

The first step for a Crucible Expedition is to select participants. The selection criteria include the demonstration of *selflessness*, a bold and *adventurous* spirit, and *heroic aspirations* to make a difference in the lives of others. Once participants are in the field, these attributes will be tested, and through the experience they will be strengthened. The challenges they face are far from abstract, whether they're being roped in on the side of a cliff, scaling slabs of red rock, leaping across icy chasms, or hunkering down in torrential hail. For some, being around others twenty-four hours a day with no downtime is emotionally exhausting. For others, the solo challenge, in which participants are asked to spend three hours alone with their thoughts, fills them with anxiety. Throughout the days and nights, the leaders exchange new ideas, and they are given a powerful opportunity to hone their leadership edge. They build resilience, resourcefulness, and new communication skills, and they create clarity for effective decision-making as they start working together.

After pushing their mental and physical abilities to the limit, the experience leaves them renewed and reinvigorated. Their growth as leaders is accelerated, accomplishing in mere days what might have taken months, or years, in a typical corporate training environment. These expeditions uncover tools the participants never realized they had at their disposal and expose them to a new understanding of what is needed to actually lead others through adversity.

Inevitably, each Crucible plays out in a similar way—whether in desert canyons or on Alaskan glaciers—with leaders striving to achieve the mission, but often failing to recognize how that singular focus can impact the commitment of the team. When real human connections are ignored, it is unlikely the team will be committed to the goals and objectives of the organization. By reorienting their priorities and focusing on the well-being of the individuals and the team, these leaders find success. In short, they discover that to go fast, they can go alone, but to go far, they must go together. Ultimately, the primary crucible lesson is *you have to slow down to speed up*.

Having run twenty-three Crucible Expeditions so far, from Argentina to Alaska, with over 250 participants, Jan has seen these leaders' transformation firsthand. Since he was nineteen years old, as a Green Beret sergeant, Jan's roles—as an instructor, business executive, professor, CEO, and expedition leader—have involved developing others. As a Green Beret, he saw that when people are confronted with serious obstacles, their true character and leadership aptitude emerge—warts and all. Combining his love for the wilderness with his passion for leadership development, in 2014, he created the Crucible Expeditions.

Jacquie participated in the Sacagawea Crucible in the Wallowa Mountains in 2018 while transitioning out of the Army. Her time in the military prepared her for the physical rigors of the Crucible, while each of her deployments—in Iraq, Afghanistan, and Syria—taught her valuable lessons she shared with the team: how to motivate and inspire soldiers, harness resources to achieve a larger mission, and build international partnerships that could have a strategic impact on United States policy. A graduate of West Point and Teachers College, Columbia University, Jacquie now blends her military experience with her rigorous academic and operational background as a leadership consultant and executive coach, helping clients from across the business community reach their goals.

Using our combined practical, academic, business, and military leadership experiences, together, we wrote this book as a way to help you overcome the many challenges faced today, not just for your own individual success, but also for that of your team members and overall organization. Here, we have translated the tactile experience of the Crucible Expedition into maxims of what it takes to lead teams. In spite of ever-present difficulties, this book aims to improve your effectiveness and create a lasting impact on the teams you lead and on your own personal and professional life. We want to inspire you to leverage the inevitable crucibles you will face so you can become mentally stronger, more aware, and the best leader you can be for those you lead.

## IT'S TIME TO CHANGE YOUR NARRATIVE

The following pages take you on a virtual journey through a Crucible Expedition to help you better understand yourself as an individual, a teammate, and a leader, while also learning how to create an environment that fosters *trust*, garners a sense of *duty*, achieves *alignment*, and sharpens *focus* on what is *truly* essential. Developing an organizational environment by design, versus default, requires you to think more like a "designer" than a "doer," but that switch isn't always easy.

Socially, culturally, and even individually, many leaders have a bias to action; we feel a need to do *something*, sometimes *anything*, even if we haven't slowed down to think it through. Instead, as a modern leader, you must set a sustainable pace that drives and renews energy into a team. Generating such sustainable energy will attract top talent who can creatively anticipate and address tomorrow's challenges, allowing you to better serve all your constituents at all levels.

Each chapter of the book, featuring quotes and stories from Crucible alumni, explores a specific step in the Crucible journey, the lessons learned from that stage of the expedition, and how those lessons can be applied in any business setting. The stories are a combination of experiences from multiple Crucibles over the years. (Aside from the epigraph attributions at the start of each chapter, the real names of participants have been changed.) You may find yourself in the mountains of Patagonia in one chapter and the glaciers of Alaska in the next, but the lessons repeat themselves on every expedition. These lessons are based around the three pillars of what we call Self-Reliant Leadership®:

- **Lead self** by assuming *ownership* and demonstrating grit.
- **Lead others** by cultivating *ownership* with a sense of duty.
- **Lead the organization** through *focus* that creates alignment.

At the end of each chapter, the takeaways are organized around these three pillars, so you can better see how each one connects to the overall themes. The self-reliant leader takes personal responsibility; assumes ownership; fulfills the obligation and responsibility for personal growth and development; demonstrates grit in the face of adversity; operates with a sense of duty toward others; and is not only self-reliant—but 100 percent reliable. Such leaders become even more effective at leading across the pillars when they understand that deliberately setting the *direction*, *pace*, and *tone* in any endeavor allows them to create the energy required for sustainable performance.

When you get the direction, pace, and tone right, you receive sustained engagement, producing a group of high performing individuals. Collectively, those individuals form a team with a common purpose, along with a compassionate sense of duty to each other. In doing so, you generate true commitment over mere compliance. Job satisfaction, well-being, engagement, home life, and performance are all positively impacted. And through the struggle, you don't just change your own narrative; you help others gain insight to envision and achieve their own aspirations.

Why should you even care about changing your narrative? Because when we're too comfortable, we don't stretch ourselves. We don't take risks or innovate. Worst of all, our personal and professional goals fall by the wayside as they lose alignment with our values. When we become complacent, we no longer strive to make a positive difference in the lives of others. And if we're not doing that, then what's the point in the first place? By changing your narrative, you turn an event or experience into information and knowledge, and that's how your own story evolves.

You are the author of your own life, but to write that story, you need to know what kind of life you want to live. This requires deep introspection, which often comes from an opportunity to pressure test yourself. We can all recall those tough times, and how they tempered, hardened, toughened, and strengthened us. They may have been physical, mental, or emotional. It could have been a lost job, a failed initiative, or even a wilderness expedition that removed you from all the creature comforts of modern life. You can initiate and design your own crucible, whether starting a social enterprise, learning a language, taking a gap year, or turning your side hustle into a full-time gig. Still, without taking the time to recognize what's been gained through this struggle, you may not have gained anything at all.

You cannot depend on others to fully prepare you for what lies ahead. The responsibility does not belong to your family, friends, school, employer, or a governmental entity. Your obligation for your future impact is your own personal responsibility. That's not to say you will go through this alone. Real human relationships are the foundation for teamwork, and they will get you beyond the next hurdle and past the next hump. Trusting others you lead, and being trusted by the same people, is paramount in any endeavor. It is our deepest hope that the following chapters help you understand how, and why, to develop that trust, and give you the persistence, passion, and determination for the crucibles in your future.

CHAPTER 1

# SELECTION

## *Selecting the Right People vs. the Best People*

> "Make sure you have good humans on the team. You can't have a high performing team with a bad person, because they will inevitably compromise and contaminate the team."
>
> —*Courtney Wilson, Veteran Participant, Moab, Utah*

Kevin was convinced he had the perfect partner for his first wilderness expedition. Who wouldn't want to be teamed up with a Special Forces soldier, a person who had been tried and tested under extreme physical, mental, and emotional conditions in some of the harshest environments? Joel's demeanor, confidence, and demonstrated survival skills from his time overseas in austere environments thoroughly impressed Kevin. In fact, Kevin even bragged to some of his colleagues at the office that he was going to have the best partner when he headed out on this "leadership, wilderness experience." He was completely confident he and Joel would make a great team, and he was already hoping it would be the beginning of a lifelong friendship. With Kevin's novice status in the wilderness, he knew Joel's strengths would complement his deficiencies, and hopefully, vice versa.

Out in the Wallowa Mountains of eastern Oregon on a crisp, sunny morning, it took less than one hour, maybe even just a matter of minutes, for Kevin to realize that he may have the best partner, but he did not have the right partner—at least not for him. It was that perfect time of year, the end of spring and cusp of summer, the weather just right. The snow had melted, the sun was high in the sky, the trail was dry, and the terrain wasn't too rugged. External conditions were perfect, but internally, Kevin struggled from the start of the steep incline up the mountain.

It was obvious things weren't going well. The group had to stop multiple times to allow Kevin to catch his breath. Eventually, the group put him up front to set a slower pace and not feel the pressure of falling behind. Joel, on the other hand, an exceptional physical specimen, was at a loss for how to work with Kevin.

In his military experience, Joel had only worked with people who could and would endure any discomfort. He was used to teammates who could suffer, dig deep, and were always prepared so their teammates could count on them. To Joel, Kevin seemed unwilling to put in the effort and "embrace the suck"—an oft-repeated phrase in the military when motivating oneself or one's team through difficult tasks in the most unpleasant circumstances. Kevin was unprepared for the trek physically and mentally. Still, Joel tried to motivate him through what he saw as words of encouragement, phrases he used often to great effect in the military: "I know you can dig deeper!" "You can always do ten times more than you think you can!" "Focus on the pain so hard it disappears into a little ball, and then throw it away!" But what Kevin heard from Joel was disappointment, contempt, and criticism. He felt like Joel thought he wasn't willing to be uncomfortable, or wasn't trying hard enough. Though Joel didn't recognize it, empathy and compassion were not necessarily his strong suit, and he was totally unaware of how his words were landing.

Compounding the situation was the fact that Joel was highly assertive, whereas Kevin was highly deferential. Highly assertive people can be difficult to influence, and others may feel overpowered or afraid to share opinions with them. Highly deferential people can become passive, resigned, or reluctant to act or share their ideas. This combination of a highly assertive person and a highly deferential person, without awareness or intention, can make for poor communication and collaboration, affecting the team dynamic in morale-draining ways. Further, when leaders are both assertive and "expert" in a domain, they often aren't open to listening to feedback from their teams. Meanwhile, a deferential person, expert or not, may take all the advice given without contextualizing it to ensure it fits the situation.

Because they were in two opposite frames of mind, there was no feedback loop for Kevin and Joel to acknowledge their areas of strength and opportunities for growth, which would have helped improve their ability to communicate and build trust. Instead, this pair found themselves unable to work together and optimize their shared accountability, causing the team to falter instead of reaching its full potential. The team's pace continued to slow, and they arrived at base camp after dark, as it was starting to rain. It was a far from ideal way to rest up for the following day's push to the summit of a 13,000-foot mountain.

When people don't communicate and collaborate well, they affect each other's drive and the morale of the entire team. The "bad vibe" between two people also acts like a contagion that infects the team's overall mood. And when people are wet, cold, and tired, they can be less than patient with each other—the opposite of effective team building. Sure, there are plenty of lessons to be learned in hindsight, but the situation hurts forward progress in the moment.

Attracting and selecting the *right* people—not necessarily the *best* people—is one of the most important skills a leader can develop as a way to improve an organization's culture and performance. The right people are those whose values, assumptions, beliefs, and expectations align with the company's core values. The best people might be the smartest, strongest, fastest, and most experienced, but their values, assumptions, beliefs, and expectations might not be in alignment with that of the organization. If that's the case, they're not the right people for your team. The right people still need to have the appropriate experience and qualifications, but selection goes much deeper. When you pick the right people over the best people, you create a competitive advantage by assembling an indomitable team with individual diversity and strength, not simply a group of great individuals.

What you appreciate in team members' performance will be an outgrowth of your organization's values. These values must therefore be made clear, concise, and easy to remember. Values need to be tied to observable behaviors if you have any hope of making them drive actions, decisions, and performance. Hiring is a critical time to start building an understanding of what those values mean in the way the team functions. By hiring and retaining team members who are on the same page, a relentless pursuit of a defined vision can carry on unabated.

## CRITERIA FOR SELECTION

You've likely heard the following said by one or more of your bosses: "We need to have more ownership and accountability around here!" It's a common refrain of many executives, specifically when tasks aren't getting done and goals aren't being accomplished. The result is disappointment, not just by the leaders but by the employees as well. Disappointment leads to frustration and dysfunction on all fronts. But often, the real issue isn't accountability; the real issue is that ownership was never possible because expectations weren't set in the first place. What is truly valued when it comes to performance, and the specific observable behaviors that display those values, is not often clearly established by senior executives during the selection or hiring process.

When observable behaviors are identified, it's much easier to provide clarity for expectations, and to let people know where they stand, thereby creating the basis for accountability. Examples of such behavior might include responsiveness for service, well-timed questions for communication, and promises kept when it comes to collaborating with others. Those observable behaviors can even be the main criteria for selection, as each supports specific values, such as reliability or punctuality.

The selection process for a Crucible Expedition is no different: each value that makes for a great team, and an excellent participant, can be seen through specific behaviors. The criteria for selection are what determines how high the bar can be raised. Establishing clear criteria leads to successful performance as part of an indomitable team. A high performing team might have different functions, and goals, but the focus on results is the same: selecting the right team members is foundational to creating a group that trusts each other, and is willing to work diligently toward a defined common purpose.

For the Crucible Expeditions, selection is based around three core values:

- Selflessness
- Adventurous spirit
- Heroic aspirations

Let's take a deep dive into each one of these values and the corresponding observable behaviors. By understanding each value, you can begin developing your own framework for the selection criteria specific for the position you're hiring for, the team you're building, and the company culture you're developing.

### *Selflessness*

When it comes to selflessness, look for people who believe *we* comes before *me*. This axiom manifests itself in a sense of duty and responsibility to the team. It's critical that leaders are humble enough to be led by others when the situation warrants it, recognizing when someone else has more insight, experience, or skill to provide collective guidance. But selflessness can also be seen in smaller ways, like when someone pitches in without being asked, collaborates openly, helps others shine, and generally puts the needs of the team before those of their own. Such people are resilient, able to adapt based on new information that results from obstacles, challenges, issues, and problems. They need to be a real contributor to the team's success. These are people who take personal responsibility for their own growth and development, and assume ownership for the overall outcome of the team. They are both leaders and excellent followers.

Considering this expectation of selflessness, you can extract the following observable behaviors as criteria for selection:

- **Initiative.** Do you, as the leader, always have to prompt teammates and ask for volunteers, or are teammates chiming in to offer their talents and knowledge in support of the team? You want folks who are proactive, not just reactive. They must be problem identifiers as much as they are problem-solvers.
- **Collaborative.** Do teammates regularly reach out to each other to gain alternative perspectives? Do teammates respond when someone asks for their help? These types of people readily ask for help by setting aside their pride and ego.
- **Adaptable.** In today's dynamic environment, are teammates able to pivot as needed in order to effectively react to changing situations? They must be open-minded about changing their priorities and comfortable with some things being perfect whereas others might need to be just so-so.

- **Resilient.** Are teammates able to persevere through hardships while performing at a high level without burning out? They must understand the difference between what they can control, what they can influence, and what is not within their control or influence.
- **Driven.** Are teammates ready to tackle the next mountain? Are they constantly learning, growing, and pushing themselves and each other? They have to be curious about how the little things are critical to the big picture.
- **Prepared.** Do teammates arrive ready to deliver on expectations, having done the proper research, collaboration, and problem-solving ahead of time? They need to allocate openings in their calendar so they have time to prepare for meetings and time after meetings to follow up.
- **Responsive.** Are teammates able to prioritize effectively so as to be responsive to the most urgent tasks required, thus accepting that other tasks must be delegated or deprioritized? These team members understand that compressing time to create efficiencies is a major competitive advantage for the organization.

### *Adventurous Spirit*

To find and select those with an adventurous spirit, seek out people who are bold and willing to take calculated risks. These are team members who are comfortable with being uncomfortable, physically and emotionally. Though they may possess a certain amount of swagger, they must also be vulnerable and humble when it comes to having their views challenged. They should be open to the opportunity of legitimate criticism. A major indicator of an adventurous spirit is a genuine curiosity that shows up as an insatiable thirst for knowledge, experiences, and challenges, which point to the real path of growth. In other words, they need to have a willingness to leave their comfort zone.

Observable behaviors for an adventurous spirit include:

- **Confidence.** Without being arrogant, do teammates constantly hone their competencies, and are they able to share them with the team?
- **Risk tolerance.** Do teammates effectively analyze and understand risk, allowing them to make balanced decisions about which risks have the potential to solve a problem or gain a competitive advantage?
- **Authenticity.** Are teammates able to show their weaknesses, or do they hide vulnerabilities, which could create big problems for the team when faced with challenges where strengths are absent and weaknesses aren't anticipated?
- **Undaunted.** Whether afraid or not, do your teammates still push forward, knowing that difficulties are to be expected?
- **Positivity.** In spite of all of the difficulties and challenges, are your teammates able to maintain a positive attitude, knowing that negativity is a contagion from within, one that can be far more detrimental than an external threat?

### *Heroic Aspirations*

Heroic aspirations are present in people with drive and ambition, and in those who find deep purpose and meaning in leveraging their natural born and acquired talents in service to others. Their aspirations go far beyond power and money. This value manifests itself in big, audacious goals that can only be achieved over a long period of time, and through the enlistment of people's time, energy, and effort. Heroic aspirations cannot be reached without influencing others, which ties back to the value of selflessness.

The observable behaviors for heroic aspirations include:

- **Strategic thinking.** Can your teammates see where the organization is trying to go in the short, medium, and long term to help drive sustainable success?
- **Competitive.** The playing field is often crowded with others interested in taking your market share—do your teammates seek to gain and maintain a competitive edge?
- **Tenacious.** Are your teammates able to fully commit to achieving the goals set, regardless of setbacks? Are they determined to persist against the odds?
- **Influential.** Do your teammates leverage their power to influence others in order to achieve the set goal?
- **Ambitious.** Do your teammates settle for small wins, or do they drive toward big goals, even if those goals are audacious?

## *Two Essential Traits: Drive and Curiosity*

In addition to the values and observable behaviors described above, there are two traits that are necessary when selecting participants for any endeavor, both of which you must also consider: drive and curiosity. *Drive* is when someone assumes ownership and remains dedicated, ambitious, competitive, and motivated to achieve an objective, especially longer-term goals. *Curiosity* is the thirst for knowledge and self-improvement, the ultimate fulcrum for balancing confidence and humility, and the key to being a good listener and collaborating with others. Together, drive and curiosity create desire—the desire to develop, learn, and succeed.

The reason you must hire for these two traits is because they simply take too long, and are incredibly hard, to develop in others. As a matter of fact, one of the founders of the guide service used during the Crucible Expeditions often says, "You can't coach desire." Instilling desire in others is not the same as motivating them. Leaders can certainly create an environment where people are motivated, but as research from American psychologist Frederick Herzberg, dating back to the 1960s, shows, achievement, responsibility, growth, and the work itself are the intrinsic motivators.[1] Pay, work conditions, bosses, and peers are hygiene factors. These factors can't motivate per se—they can only demotivate if they aren't at the level expected.

Pay attention to the questions candidates ask in the selection process where curiosity is demonstrated. But you must be clear to your people that it is their individual responsibility to find purpose and meaning in their particular role. Horst Schulze, the founder of the Ritz-Carlton, once said that every employee may have a different function, but every employee has the same purpose: "Get and keep customers."[2] A door person at the Ritz, whose function is to "open and close the door," might realize that purpose by putting guests in a great mood with a friendly greeting as they start a day of meetings. Their friendliness could actually improve the chance for the success of those meetings for the people who had the privilege of passing through that particular door! The point is to help people find purpose and meaning in their work, no matter their function, that produces an uncommon focus in all areas of their responsibilities.

The bottom line is that you need people who take responsibility for their growth and will find deep personal meaning in their work and the work of the organization. With that passion comes the curiosity to understand the true downstream effect and value of the work they provide, and a determination to always up their game when it comes to being competent, confident, and collaborative. There is no substitute for a team member who is driven and curious, because they are game changers who remain in a constant state of honing their strengths. They also make adjustments with regard to where those strengths can derail them—known as weaknesses—and maintain their desire for continuous improvement.

The selection criteria provide the clarity required to ultimately assess competencies acquired through knowledge and experiences to best predict future performance. Selection criteria must match expectations for results, production, and interpersonal behaviors. You cannot see or manage what people think, feel, and believe. You can only manage what you observe—the words, deeds, and actions of others—with your own two eyes and ears.

Ensure that you set the expectations for the words, deeds, and actions of your teammates through both clear communication and modeling of the values you require. The values described above are those that are important for the high performing teams we select for Crucible Expeditions, but they may or may not serve your teams in the same way. Take the time to determine what values are essential for performance on your teams and in your unique organization.

## THE SELECTION PROCESS

When there is alignment for selection across the organization, you actually set and establish expectations during the first phases of the interview process. This sort of clarity with regard to what you value, along with your vision and mission, can also present a more favorable picture of your organization to a candidate who may be considering other options besides you.

A recent client showed us a job description they were particularly proud of, but noted that it was receiving little traction from prospective candidates. We quickly saw why: it felt stale, overly corporate, and vague (which is how many job descriptions tend to come across). The job description defined the skills and experience that were required for the role—what college degree was needed, computer skills expected, and similar material—but the description didn't explain why the role was important to the organization, nor why the position actually mattered. The corporate client was setting himself up to receive candidates who looked great on paper, but would not necessarily be the right cultural fit, nor might they be fulfilled in the company because of misaligned values.

What the executive should have been focused on were the "must have" attributes they were looking for, as opposed to just skills, and how the position fit into the larger vision of where the organization was going. While it is probably true that in most roles there is a requirement for a minimum level of skill, or even education, it is likely that hundreds of people can check those boxes. But let's assume you are looking for a unique fit for your team.

For example, the following are attributes that typically help people get promoted (and the absence of which get people demoted or terminated): tenacious, collaborative, adaptable, influential, and "gets office politics." Those phrases aren't usually contained in a corporate job description, but these traits were what the executive actually required.

## *Step-by-Step*

To decide on the observable behaviors that align with your values, you must develop specific criteria by which to evaluate, compare, and select candidates for the team. It's then critical to ensure the criteria are made clear to managers, interviewers, and human resources. The next step is to develop questions that will help determine if the applicants meet the criteria so you can begin interviewing. As explained by Bradford D. Smart, PhD, in *Topgrading: The Proven Hiring and Promoting Method That Turbocharges Company Performance*[3] (the bible for selecting and hiring), there also needs to be a process by which all the team members involved in interviewing and deciding are on the same page. The best approach is to clarify the selection process for all parties involved, breaking it down as such:

- Define the selection process by which you will reach consensus.
- Gather the facts, such as how big the pool of candidates is and where you might find people who align with your values (for example, selfless, adventurous, and possess heroic aspirations).
- Define who is involved in the decision, including the managers in the chain of command, human resources, and possibly support staff like executive assistants and those employees the candidate will need to work alongside.
- Clarify who has the actual authority to make various selection decisions. Define which decisions, based on the responsibility, impact, and dollars, can be made by whom. Such clarity will prevent bottlenecks that would be created if all decisions were to go to one person or one small group. Generate options for sourcing a list of candidates.
- Perform a cultural interview. A cultural interview, as part of the process, begins to uncover the values a candidate holds while also helping them understand more about your organization. Cultural interviews are your opportunity to set expectations around culture before teammates join, so it is essential the interview team has clarity on what they are looking for and how they will determine if values align.
- Analyze the candidates using a scorecard for the necessary attributes. For example, a score of one to five for qualifications and alignment with each of the criteria you have developed.
- Select the right candidate.
- Evaluate the choice by predicting potential difficulties assimilating, and take steps to mitigate stumbling blocks to the performance expected.
- Communicate the decision (make the offer) and take action. Communicate to the entire team that part of onboarding is making new team members feel truly welcomed, which is the opposite of a typical onboarding process that is stiff, cold, and rigid.

This process is about garnering a deeper understanding of how your candidates like to work, what their values are, and how those values align with or enhance your company culture. When the organization is aligned around hiring in this way, there is very little second-guessing on hiring the right people. No teammate should be brought on board who clearly has the skills to amplify the organization but is not a cultural fit.

### *The Interview Is a Two-Way Street*

Kelli, an active-duty Army officer, found a quiet nook in the Speaker's balcony in the United States Capitol Building to steal away for her Crucible interview ahead of engagements with members of Congress on behalf of the Army. She wasn't sure what to expect during the call, but understanding the values of the team and inferring some of the selection criteria, she had given some thought to her own "heroic aspirations." As she stared out over the National Mall, seeing the Washington Monument towering over the rest of the city, she wondered if she was worthy of the opportunity for which she was about to be interviewed. Was she of a high enough caliber to add value to the team of executives who would be out on the trek? Were her goals lofty enough to be described as "heroic"?

The phone rang. Despite her nerves, she was committed to making a positive impression. The interview questions asked were not the typical ones she anticipated as she prepared to leave the Army. While Kelli felt unprepared for the questions around her aspirations, the questions that really challenged her involved her willingness to leave her comfort zone and be vulnerable during the expedition. Although her self-doubt created some internal tension, Kelli was excited about the opportunity to be a part of a team that wanted to explore the answers to questions about purpose, values, what it means to serve, and how one defines a good life.

As the conversation continued, she later said, it felt as much like a soul-searching session as it did an interview. She knew value alignment and like-minded participants were needed to ultimately forge a high performing team. The interview was far from academic or sterile, and that's how she knew she wanted in. She was looking forward to being part of something special, and the interview itself created the expectation that she had to be emotionally and mentally prepared so as not to let the team down in any way.

When selecting teammates for the Crucible, many "best people" are bypassed in search of the few "right people." It is easy to become distracted by resumes of achievement and pedigree, but your future team is counting on you to select a group who will collectively become a high performing team. Any interview can be crafted to create a unique process that instills an instant level of understanding among the teammates when they later prepare to venture "into the wilderness together"—literally in the case of the Crucible, and figuratively in the case of colleagues facing unexpected challenges.

An effective interview process is a two-way street, and shows candidates the why. It sets the tone for how it will feel to be part of something different, exciting, and bigger than themselves. And if selected, they feel as if they have already passed the first test, and start to feel an instant level of trust with other teammates. They recognize everyone was chosen for shared values and similar, but diverse, experiences. That feeling translates to an obligation to perform at a high level, and bring their unique perspective as a value add to strengthen the team.

The Crucible, by its very nature, attracts leaders who self-select because they want to do more than learn how to better lead others. They want to enrich themselves, evolve, and hone their leadership edge. In general, people seek a higher purpose, and that aspiration needs to shine like a beacon to attract the right suitors. When hiring, leaders often just look for candidates who fit the job description by possessing certain qualifications, and seem personable enough. They're looking for three basic things: Can this person do the job? Do I like him or her? Does he or she like me? It really is that simple. But that simplistic approach is not going to cut it for the rigors of an expedition, or the challenges organizations face in today's uncertain world.

## ONGOING SELECTION PROCESS

When the traits you interview for are observable behaviors, those behaviors will inform how you manage and lead going forward. Keep in mind, you might value integrity and loyalty, but unless you've figured out the observable behaviors that align with integrity and loyalty, there won't be clear expectations. When you hire someone, it is a reflection of what you value. If that employee doesn't work out, you will probably be reluctant to fire the person you hired in the first place. Frankly, your ego gets in the way. But it's unrealistic to think you can *never* make a hiring mistake. Just because someone was successful at another organization at another time does not necessarily mean they will experience the same level of success with the unique challenges at your organization. Nor is it guaranteed they will perform to your standard. Further, even if someone is a perfect fit the day you hire them, this does not mean they will still be a perfect fit a year, or three years, from now.

People change. Some constantly learn; some don't. Markets change. The environment presents new challenges, and organizations must adapt. That's why leaders need to constantly interpret what's going on outside the organization to determine what must take place inside the organization. Externally, they need to make time for customers so they can see patterns and trends and assess competitive threats. Internally, they must define a high performing team and uphold the values and standards by which goals are attained. The results must come from individual contribution, collective teamwork, and organizational collaboration.

In the best organizations, selection is therefore an ongoing process. It's the athletic equivalent of making the team roster every year. It's about every member of the team keeping up with new people who might be faster, stronger, smarter, and more energetic. It's about being hungry, driven, curious, and relentless. For the expeditions, that means using the same observable behaviors to select a team as the expectation and standard of performance for the team. As the leader, you set this climate for your team when you constantly ensure that people are growing and developing their competence with regard to translating knowledge into skill, and skill into behavior. This creates a proven path for individual success and team performance. By selecting the right people for your team, versus who others might consider the best people, you ensure that you maintain the culture that best supports your organization's values and successful implementation of your strategy.

**PRO TIP**

Don't stop with simply identifying and defining your values. Get granular with the behaviors you expect to see at different levels of responsibility and tenure within your team. At West Point, the Honor Code, "A Cadet will not lie, cheat, steal, or tolerate those who do," is taught and rigidly enforced. If a cadet violates the code, they face consequences, the severity depending on their years as a cadet. Expectations vary and evolve, but values do not.

▲▲▲

Now take a moment to consider your own organization and how you approach selection:

- How do you align your hiring committee on the values, attributes, and characteristics that are most important for the role and the team?

- Do your requirements narrow the field of qualified applicants in such a way that you can still attract a diverse group of candidates?
- How do you create an environment where people understand they are always expected to live up to the selection criteria?

## THE REST OF THE STORY

Back to Kevin and Joel, 13,000 feet up the side of the mountain. Kevin struggled physically the rest of the trip, but he dug deep thanks to his teammates' encouragement, and he rallied on the last day, making the final trek without slowing the team's pace. He found the motivation he needed, in part due to the obligation he felt to the team. During the evening debrief, his teammates were brutally honest with him. They conveyed that he had been selfish. He was selected with a certain expectation for performance, and he had not adequately prepared, which changed the trip for the entire team. The pace was slower, the alternate route selected was easier, and certain goals were eliminated, taking away their chance to make it to a summit and feel the exhilaration of their accomplishment. There's nothing like looking out across that mountain range and seeing the crystal blue water of Wallowa Lake below.

Kevin said he valued fitness and health, but he was spending twelve to sixteen hours a day at work, subsisting on fast food for almost every meal. Where he was spending his time did not match up to what he said he valued earlier in the trip. During the debrief, he made a commitment to himself—and the group—that he would work to get in better shape, knowing that doing so would give him the energy he needed to be a better and healthier husband and father—and a better teammate back at the office, too.

As for Joel, in the weeks that followed the Crucible, he realized his personal crucible hadn't been the physical part of the expedition, but the interpersonal part. The Crucible had a lingering effect as he continued to reflect on how he needed to adapt from the mindset of a military warrior to the mindset that performance is not just results, but behaviors aligned with core values. He would need to adapt to the business environment in which he was now entering.

In both cases, Kevin and Joel realized they had stepped out of their comfort zones and into a crucible. Rather than let the Crucible break them down, they persisted. They were selected for their values and similar, but diverse, experiences. The result showed how important it is to align expectations from the outset, which is what it means to select the "right" people.

## CONCLUSION

The selection process sets the stage for what will, and will not, be the standard of performance for your team. Creating the right culture must be deliberate, and it starts at selection. Each time you uphold your values, you forge and reinforce the makings of an indomitable team. When you let standards slip—even just once—you erode the trust of the team, which is the true foundation of success.

Setting the culture you want begins with selection, but it doesn't end with hiring the right people. The decisions you make on a daily basis, the incentives by which you reinforce certain attributes, and the consequences for disruptive behavior are what make selection sticky. Selection isn't something that just happens when new people join the team; selection is an ongoing process by which standards are upheld and culture is treated not just as a word, but something that people internalize as a duty to accomplish heroic aspirations.

## THE THREE PILLARS

### *Leading Self*

Personal reflection on what values are most important to you is critical in building a trustworthy team that performs. You must be personally committed to these values and able to role model them.

- What are your top values, and are you able to articulate how they align with those of the team?
- How do you demonstrate your commitment to the values, and expectations, set by the organization?
- Who are you seeking feedback from to improve your self-awareness?

### *Leading Others*

Select people based on what values, attributes, and traits you hold dear. Remember, each team member is key to the dynamic of a high performing team.

- What observable behaviors do you expect based on the core values?
- How do you communicate the expectations of observable behaviors to your teammates?
- What mechanisms do you have in place to ensure accountability to shared values?

### *Leading the Organization*

A relentless pursuit of vision means assembling the right people for the team.

- How do you communicate the skill level required for a new team member versus a senior member so that there is still perceived fairness?
- Are there sacred cows in your organization? If so, what can be done to uphold the standards fairly?
- Have you established clear criteria for the decision-making process involved in selection, and are they understood throughout the organization?

CHAPTER 2

# PREPARATION

## *Getting Squared Away*

> "I told myself that I knew I could do it; I just needed courage."
>
> —*Jay Packard, Executive Participant, Dominguez Canyon, Colorado*

The hike was 7.5 miles uphill in the Wallowa Mountains of eastern Oregon. The mountains abut Idaho, near where Lewis and Clark crossed on their way to the Pacific Ocean over two hundred years ago. It's still a place where you might be lucky enough to hear wolves howl at night. Steep mountains stretch as far as the eye can see. Unusually lush and heavily vegetated terrain is dotted with crystal clear lakes that remain frigid even in the summer. The access points are far from the nearest interstate highways, so there are no crowds like those found in national parks, and thus, the Wallowas retain a certain wildness uncommon in today's lower forty-eight states.

As the group climbed, everyone sized each other up. Some tried to establish themselves as the alpha of the pack, rushing ahead, grunting with each long stride; others simply attempted, and failed, to not look tired already. Bill, a middle-aged executive from a Fortune 500 financial firm, had not gone hiking since Boy Scouts. Not only did he mention he had too much weight on his back, he also openly admitted he had too much weight on his body. About halfway up to the first camp, he started looking more than a little peaked. Instead of stopping to take a break, drink some water, and personally regroup, he decided to power through. That's when he projectile vomited in the middle of the trail. Everyone in the group froze, stunned at the sight of their teammate launching his lunch—the meal they had just shared before beginning the climb—three feet in front of himself.

Most of the participants seemed unsure of what to do. After a moment, someone offered Bill water, while others quietly wondered aloud if they would need to help carry him back down the trail. But Angie, a petite woman who had been hiking next to Bill, was the first one to offer real help.

Angie, who holds a PhD in physics and is an accomplished mountaineer, deftly approached Bill and offered to switch backpacks. Bill's was a bulky, frame-heavy relic from the 1970s; hers was sleek and new, the size of a seven-year-old's book bag. It took about three seconds for Bill to humbly accept the offer. He recognized that if he didn't, the rest of the trip would be quite the experience both for him and his teammates—and not a good one. He could increasingly become a liability. More importantly, that selfless act of kindness reinforced why Bill was there, why they were all there: to not only challenge themselves, but to build a cohesive team in the process.

Though Bill had believed he was ready for the trek, he simply wasn't prepared. And whether you're getting ready for an expedition, starting a project, taking on a new team, or realigning an existing one, *preparation is everything.* As an individual member of the team, you need to take personal responsibility for that preparation. But as a leader, you also need to help your team to be ready for the challenges ahead. Therefore, preparation must allow the team to connect and start developing a relationship even before the expedition or project begins. This process starts with a proper welcoming and must be followed by a consistent, compelling orientation where expectations are framed and values are aligned.

The aim is to create a team that is engaged and aligned with short- and long-term goals, committed to each other, accountable for failures and mistakes, and selfless in action. The result is a team that has a common purpose, is duty-bound to each other, team-oriented, and courageous enough to risk saying what they think. This is a team who cares deeply for one another and possesses an uncommon degree of trust. And it all starts with "getting squared away."

## GETTING SQUARED AWAY

In the military, being squared away means you can't be "late, light, or out of uniform." "Late" is pretty self-explanatory—show up on time, or you will have to deal with a few extra push-ups! "Light" means not having the required gear for the task at hand. And "out of uniform" means not being prepared for the elements. For business leaders embarking on a Crucible Expedition, it's much the same. They must arrive on time. They have to bring the required gear and clothing for the given climate and expedition. And most importantly of all, they need to be able to support their fellow team members.

If you arrive to a meeting late, unprepared to discuss the topic at hand—a pile of papers at your side with no rhyme or reason, or an incomprehensible slide deck on a flash drive—you're of course hurting yourself, but in the process, you're hurting your team, too. Your problem has now become theirs, and the trust you are hoping to instill falters. Being squared away allows others to rely on you. When you're squared away, you demonstrate selflessness. On the Crucible, you have all your gear in order, you're physically fit, you're present, you're in a receptive frame of mind, and most importantly, you are there to help your team members when needed. When everyone on a team follows suit, trust begins to rapidly develop among the group.

Consider Bill again: though it might be unfair to say he was acting selfishly, his lack of preparation certainly affected the other participants. Luckily, Angie was prepared. Her fitness and forethought allowed her to help Bill, and in the process, trust was built among the entire team as everyone learned they could rely on each other if the need arose. Though Bill was embarrassed, this mini-crisis provided the first opportunity for the group to rally as a team, not just as a loose gaggle of individuals.

Angie demonstrated integrity and the ability to be trusted, values that must be backed by actual behaviors, such as selflessness and reliability. As highlighted in chapter one, you can throw around words like "integrity" and "trust," but unless those values are supported through action, they are just talking points and flowery language. By being squared away, Angie's ability and willingness to help changed the course of everyone's experience.

### *Three Levels to Being Squared Away*

When leading a business or group at the highest level, you must be squared away. This takes a combination of self-discipline and intentional sacrifice, which can be broken down into categories: physical, mental and emotional, and relational. These categories are necessary for the team to gain an uncommon commitment to each other and the journey ahead, no matter what it may be—and no matter the level of leadership.

#### Physical

Months before they arrive for the expedition, most leaders who head out on a Crucible recognize they are not necessarily physically prepared to begin their journey. Those who are truly committed to the experience, though, ask for physical training plans, exercises they can do, and advice early on. Ben was just one of those leaders.

Years earlier, when he was in his physical prime, Ben spent a lot of time in the mountains—hiking, climbing, exploring—but over the years those excursions had tapered off. He knew he was going to be putting his body to the test on his upcoming Crucible in South America, and he was afraid he wouldn't be able to keep up during the expedition. He recognized that if he trailed behind the rest of the team, he'd be letting them down.

So, after speaking with a physical trainer, months ahead of the Crucible, Ben started walking long distances on the weekends, wearing the pack he'd be using. Over the weeks, he continued to increase the weight in his pack, even beyond what he would be carrying on the expedition. Since the terrain he had available to him in Chicago paled in comparison to what he would encounter in Patagonia, that extra weight helped him get a better feel for what the trek would actually be like on his shoulders and feet.

In the business world, no one is expecting you to physically train like you're going out on a hard-core expedition, but taking care of yourself is crucial. Truth be told, though, it's hard. We all know what to do—eat right, exercise, reduce stress, get enough rest—but our physical fitness often takes a back seat to the seemingly endless personal and professional responsibilities, tasks, and obligations we deal with every day. It would be great to take a forty-five-minute break to hit the gym, or a half hour to cook a healthy meal at home, but that's a combined hour and fifteen minutes that we might think is better served responding to emails, returning client calls, and checking in on that thorny project's progress.

You need time to take care of yourself, to build resilience and prepare for the obstacles ahead. As burnout continues to increase, in spite of the attention it's received—especially in the hybrid and work-from-home environments—it's important to stop and spend a moment to take stock of how your physical preparedness, or lack thereof, is affecting you, and those around you.

For example, a founder and CEO of a medium-sized defense contractor believed he recognized the value of physical fitness. He went for walks every day, typically followed by long bike rides. On the weekends, he made it a family affair, and he and his wife could be seen out on their bikes on Saturdays and Sundays, riding for twenty or more miles. He also ate healthily and didn't drink. All in all, you would think he was the perfect picture of health. But then he hit a wall, right in the middle of an acquisition. No matter how much he focused on diet and exercise, he just couldn't find the stamina he needed in order to help lead his company through it.

When asked about his sleep habits, he proudly stated he was able to function well on five hours a night—an obvious red flag. He was encouraged to buy a fitness tracker to track his sleep and recovery. The resulting data told a different story about the impact of his sleep habits. He made a commitment to shift his evening routine to get at least seven hours of sleep every night. Once he followed through on this commitment, he found the energy and mental focus he needed to effectively lead his team and company. If he hadn't taken an extra two hours a night to simply get some rest, his overall effectiveness would have continued to be wholly diminished.

Physical readiness is the tide that raises all boats. If you make fitness and physical wellness a priority, you will find you are also better prepared to take care of other aspects of your well-being, including the state of your mental and emotional health. This helps you remain predictable and reliable to the people you're privileged to, and entrusted with, serving.

## Mental and Emotional

Being squared away mentally and emotionally means you do the requisite self-care so your personal affairs are in order and you have a clear mind to focus on the task at hand. For example, too often on a Crucible, leaders share that they neglect family matters, with work always taking priority. Children's baseball games and dance recitals are missed with a promise of "next time," while the boss and colleagues only hear, "Yes, I will be there," or "Yes, I will get it done." A cloudy, distracted mind takes away the concentration needed to successfully prepare for, and complete, an expedition, to be there for teammates, and to maintain safety. If participants arrive unprepared and unable to give the expedition their full attention, the results can be dire.

To that end, team members on the Crucible are expected to do some necessary pre-work before they arrive. They must read assigned articles on adversity, diversity, and what others have learned from similar expeditions into the wilderness. They are required to participate in multiple preparation calls. And they are encouraged to reflect on their personal strengths and weaknesses through a behavioral survey that considers over one hundred soft skills. The self-reflection is an opportunity for participants to see where their strengths have served them heretofore, and where those same strengths might detract from new, higher levels of responsibility. It's also important for participants to view the maps and routes to gain familiarity with the terrain, elevation gain, weather, water sources, and gear required. This knowledge allows them to consider what obstacles they may need to mentally and emotionally prepare for, such as exposure to heights.

This foundational understanding of key material helps in developing a shared purpose among the group, accelerating a common sense of trust. Pre-work allows team-time together to be spent discussing what they hope to get out of the experience and the challenges and issues they're facing. They can then collaborate on potential solutions. In this way, they build trust with their partners, and come prepared with a head start on relationships and the critical component of trust.

In general, individuals who work hard to build relationships, and create a sense of duty to one another, sow the seeds for what becomes a high performing team. As a result, more meaningful relationships are formed. The profound impact on both the preparatory connection between teammates and their ideas cannot be understated. For example, when preparation for meetings does not happen, they're a waste of everyone's time and energy, and should therefore be canceled. As Joe Allen, the co-author of *Suddenly Hybrid: Managing the Modern Meeting*, says, "One bad meeting causes three more meetings."[1]

Josh, a senior executive with a multibillion-dollar manufacturing company, admitted to the group, "I'm a natural planner and a *Nervous Nellie*." Given these tendencies, he was anxious about the trip. It was understandable. He'd be away from work for days. His company was having a rough time meeting customer demands, his people were stretched thin, and future success was anything but certain. This situation led him to be concerned about taking time off to embark on the Crucible for the promise of what *might* come out of the experience, when he *knew* he was needed back in the office. He was, however, committed to the process, the adventure, the team—and he was not going to back out.

Josh had to not only prepare himself to unplug from work and contribute to the Crucible team, but he needed to ensure that his work team was truly engaged in his absence. He wanted them to be confident in their ability to handle anything that may arise while he was unreachable. (There's no cell signal 12,000 feet up in the Rocky Mountains.) Therefore, he deliberately set the stage weeks in advance by creating opportunities for other leaders to sit in on meetings, talk through decisions, and discuss the external environment. This approach would allow those leaders to see how he made decisions and set expectations for acceptable levels of risk. In the process, Josh mentally prepared both himself and his team for his trip, empowering others to take control in his absence. Their confidence allowed him to be mentally and emotionally all in while hiking through the breathtaking mountains of Colorado.

## Relational

The third level to getting squared away is "relational." You need to arrive prepared to work with others on your team by having already laid the groundwork to develop productive, cooperative relationships. This means being open-minded and ready to work with everyone, despite some people being difficult at times (which is to be expected).

When a new team or group is created, or a new member joins, from the beginning, everyone involved needs to feel as if they belong and their voice matters. For the Crucible, participants must take individual responsibility to connect with each other one-on-one before arrival. This preparation gives them the opportunity to get to know each other's personal expectations for the program, and how they can assist each other before, during, and after the trip. In any team-building situation, the goal of such preparation is to get people to not only work *with* each other, but *for* each other.

One way to begin that process is by finding an accountability partner. An accountability partner is someone at your peer level who you trust enough to confide in, and who trusts you in return. This is someone with whom you could discuss a difficult employee, an important financial decision, or another sensitive matter not easily shared with direct reports or superiors. This relationship should allow either of you to risk saying what you truly think to help uncover blind spots. This may include pointing out your partner's over-reliance on skills that got them promoted, but no longer serve them as a leader with a higher level of responsibility. Accountability partners can either be assigned by the group leader or individuals can choose their own. These partners make it easier for people to connect, and learn to rely on each other so they're ready to work together when a new project, issue, or opportunity arises.

Remember Ben from Chicago, mentioned earlier in this chapter? Part of his physical preparation for his adventure in Patagonia included connecting with another person in the area who was going to be on the Crucible Expedition with him. When he learned that one of his teammates, Shannon, was training in the Chicago area, they linked up and began training together. This new partnership led to a shared sense of accountability and motivation even before they met the rest of the team. Such buddy hikes ensured that not only was Ben prepared, but so was Shannon. Being squared away meant that no one would have to help carry their loads.

▲▲▲

When each person within a group individually recognizes the importance of being squared away through the categories of preparation, they can improve the team dynamic and organizational environment before inevitable challenges occur. It's not always easy, and it takes time, dedication, and sacrifice, but it is your personal responsibility to ensure you carry your own weight—and then some. That's what going above and beyond means. You need to be able to rely on yourself to do the required pre-work so others can rely on you in turn. It comes down to being selfless, not selfish. As a team, company, or organizational leader, you are required to uphold the standard for others to get squared away as well.

## THE LEADER'S RESPONSIBILITY

"So, what questions do you have?"

Dead silence.

Hmm . . . aren't these leaders of Fortune 500 companies and warriors from the special operations community? Didn't some of them go to the most prestigious schools in the world, and haven't they all been filtered through various selection processes their entire careers? But none of them are speaking up. Not one of them has taken the lead to ask the "dumb" question.

This silence happens during the preparatory video call for every expedition, without fail. In part, these calls are meant to answer logistical questions about gear, transportation, food, and fitness, but their main purpose is to set a standard for behavior. Expectations need to be set when it comes to the selflessness, curiosity, open-mindedness, and noble aspirations that are required for the Crucible journey. There are usually four to five calls that take place in the six months leading up to the Crucible. The behavioral survey analysis is discussed, during which participants share how their strongest soft skills may actually produce conflict when out on the expedition (for example, assertive people being teamed up with highly deferential people, as explored with Kevin and Joel in chapter one).

During these calls, participants hold back as they feel out the group and, maybe more importantly, their place within it. They know they are in the presence of other great leaders, all of whom have just as impressive resumes and track records in leading, innovating, and making things happen. It's a rare moment of intimidation, one that will come up again when these same participants are pushed further out of their comfort zones. And, during a Crucible, they certainly are pushed.

They are teamed up with other overachieving alpha dogs and then pulled into discussions that expose their insecurities. Their vulnerability quickly surfaces, and they're forced to look inward to redefine how they balance their confidence and humility. In a wilderness environment, people bond faster, but in the preparation stage, their lack of vulnerability sets them up for possible failure. That's where the leader comes in.

The Crucible experience shows that you are the first one who has to be squared away. But once that's a focus, you are also responsible to help get your team there as well. To do so, any initial orientation for a team, project, or initiative needs to be clear and compelling. As leaders, you have to recognize whether the welcoming and orientation phase is set up to effectively support the ability of individuals and teams to properly prepare ahead of execution. During that process, you must make no assumptions, while also reducing ambiguity.

### *Make No Assumptions*

Assumptions—which are most often described as communication problems—keep us from having aligned expectations. We assume the message sent is the same as the message received. We assume people understand what we expect. That they know where they stand with us. And that they understand how their behavior affects others. We also assume projects will get done on time and under budget, and that next year will be better than the last. We assume the competition doesn't know as much as we do, and doesn't work as hard. We assume that in three weeks we will be caught up, and things will magically slow down.

Of course, our assumptions are often very wrong.

We make assumptions because we have a lifetime of experiences that can often help us speed up decision-making. But that doesn't always mean we're making the right decisions. In a complex world, we first need to slow down to validate, or invalidate, our assumptions and better understand the situation at hand. Only then can we speed up.

Humbly ask yourself, "What is the best way to eliminate assumptions so that I have more unbiased confidence in my judgment?" As a leader, you can never make assumptions about individual team members or teams as a whole. When starting a new project, for example, you will cover the basics, but you can never assume your team already has first-hand knowledge of the expected outcome, its background, or what's at stake. The fundamentals must be covered. During a Crucible, assuming the guidance and direction sent is the guidance and direction received can be disastrous.

People often think what they're saying is what the listener is actually hearing, and that's rarely the case. If you've ever explained a process to your team, and then they've gone off and done something entirely different, whose fault is that? Did you take the time to make sure everyone really understands what's going on? It never hurts to politely ask (with a smile on your face), "I'm not sure what I just said, so could you tell me what you heard?" By eliminating assumptions, you create a fearless environment where people can be open and honest, not worried they'll be chastised for asking questions. And that openness will lead to better understanding all around.

### *Reduce Ambiguity*

No matter if you're an entrepreneur, founder, author, musician, artist, or corporate or military leader, you will only be successful if you have an insatiable curiosity for figuring out why things are the way they are. And once you do, you need to discover how those things might be improved when ambiguity is reduced. You have to tinker, experiment, fail, learn, share, then try again. You have to explore. Clear expectations create a culture where people feel a duty to one another. If your team members don't know the expectations, where they stand, and the consequences of their performance, then you are not fulfilling your duties as a leader. You must therefore reduce ambiguity to help your team get squared away. That starts with a common purpose and trust.

A common purpose can only be accomplished by working together. Reaching this goal requires two metrics: the actual result, outcome, or number, and equally important, the behaviors of the group that produce the result. Those intentional behaviors form the foundation for trust. The seeds of trust can be sown through continuously improving four dynamics on your team to reduce (maybe even eliminate) ambiguity:

- **Communication.** Model curiosity. Use the power of the question to ensure you're reducing ambiguity, and evaluate your own hypotheses about the root cause of issues. Test your assumptions and hypothesis by gathering multiple points of view. This can be done by conducting surveys and asking questions of all constituents (superiors, direct reports, peers, customers, and partners). Listen intently for what's said and not said to most accurately assess and interpret confirming and disconfirming input. Further, who communicates what to who, when, and how must be crystal clear. For example, you may tell your team that you will provide a detailed update on a project's progress every Friday at 4 PM via email. But you must be predictable and also follow through on that update every week as planned.

- **Decisions.** Define which person or group has the authority to make what level of decisions, and be specific about the process by which the decision is made. For example, is it made by *consensus* or decree? Most importantly, ensure that the prioritized criteria by which the decision will be made are clear and understood by all. The criteria should reflect what you hold dear and be aligned with your group's key organizational values. On an expedition, safety is always at the top. In business, it might be profit margin, efficiency, or weighted to the most valued customers.
- **Meetings.** Keep the rules of meetings sacred so they can actually be a differentiator for supercharged collaboration. Simple rules, where violations have consequences, can work wonders, as long as everyone knows them ahead of time. For example, behaviors like tardiness, interrupting others, and not speaking up must get addressed soon after the behavior, or lack thereof, is observed. This means a leader needs to constantly uphold the standards of performance (i.e., expected behaviors). Also, consider twenty-minute or forty-five-minute meetings versus thirty- and sixty-minute meetings so people have time to prep, follow up, and even use the bathroom! No meeting should be

scheduled unless there is an objective and agenda. Further, no meeting should conclude without answering two key questions: 1) Who does what by when? 2) Who needs to communicate what to whom by when? The answer to those two questions should be in the recap, which should go out to all participants right away. (See chapter nine for a further discussion on decisions and meetings in context of a team's rhythm.)

- **Conflict.** Allow for conflict, which is inevitable and healthy in a safe and diverse environment. In advance of the project or initiative, map out with the team likely areas of conflict based on past experiences, and memorialize action steps on how inevitable conflict will be mitigated. For example, if someone is not pulling their weight, that person will be notified. If the issue doesn't improve, that person may be removed from the team. Teams that slow down to set the rules of the road do much better when conflict occurs than the teams who rush right into the work.

**PRO TIP**

Consider keeping track of assumptions and promises made in meetings. Have the person tracking those read them aloud before the meeting concludes. It's a great opportunity to identify and eliminate assumptions, including your own, and help people realize the promises or commitments they made to the team. It's also another way to solidify a sense of disciplined duty among team members.

▲▲▲

Now take a moment to consider your own organization and how you approach helping your team members get squared away:

- What assumptions do you regularly make about individuals and the team?
- Do people feel safe to ask questions, even when they "should" already know the answer?
- Are expectations so clear there is little room for ambiguity?

## THE REST OF THE STORY

At the end of the Crucible, each teammate is asked to set an ambitious yet achievable goal and commit to accomplishing it. Bill—the Wallowa Mountain participant who arrived unprepared—committed to hiking three of Colorado's 14,000-foot peaks by the end of the following year. With his own commitment and fortitude, coupled with the encouragement of his teammates, Bill exceeded his commitment and tackled *four* of Colorado's 14,000-foot peaks in the next year with his family in tow. This ambitious goal wasn't the only one that Bill walked away with from the Crucible. He committed to becoming a better leader, to put the concepts he learned on the Crucible into practice every day at work. Preparation was at the top of his list. This commitment to growth earned him a promotion, and in turn, he focused on the development and promotion of his teammates. His family also shared in his inspiring journey, and they all got "squared away" so they could accompany him on his climbs!

## CONCLUSION

The *aim* of preparation is to create momentum and a team that is engaged for the challenges to come, committed to the mission, accountable for their mistakes, selfless in their sacrifices, and duty-bound to each other. The *result* of preparation is a team that is courageous enough to say what they think, resourceful enough to know that it isn't always about more "resources," resilient to inevitable setbacks, disciplined with respect to time management, and graced with the humility to ask the dumb question. Basically, near-perfect teammates behaving rationally, predictably, and with zero drama! But alas, we are all works in progress, often with unrealistic expectations of the people we select and lead.

By getting squared away, you can begin to reach toward that utopian team ideal. As an individual, you must do your part, ensuring you're not the "sprained ankle" that throws the expedition into disarray. You must prepare ahead of time, whether joining a new team, or getting started on a new project. This means being physically, mentally and emotionally, and relationally prepared. To help others get squared away, you must be careful with assumptions, reduce ambiguity, and set clear expectations and goals. Most importantly, you have to help people discover real purpose and meaning in their role. In so doing, you create that elusive sense of duty—a shared accountability that creates uncommon, extraordinary, and high performing teams.

## THE THREE PILLARS

### *Leading Self*

Your first duty is to take responsibility and ownership for being squared away. That means being prepared in every sense of the word. You have to be self-reliant enough to trust your own abilities.

- Are you prepared to lead yourself?
- Have you invested in your well-being to meet the expectations of yourself, your team, and your organization?
- What one habit can you commit to that would allow you to be even more squared away?

### *Leading Others*

Though you can only control how you spend your time and how you respond to the environment around you, you can also influence others through your words and deeds. When you're prepared, others know they can rely on you to anticipate needs, react to the situation (and opportunity) at hand, and be there to help when necessary.

- Are you prepared to lead others?
- Have you established relationships with those who you rely on to ensure you are able to support each other when the need arises?
- Have you made clear to the team both what they need to accomplish and why it's important?

### *Leading the Organization*

Preparation certainly calls for disciplined execution, but the precursor must be an elegant design. To that end, you must foster an environment in which people know they matter, belong, and have a voice. This design is a result of being thoughtful, intentional, and purposeful. Ensure that selection and preparation are consistent and the result will be teams who are engaged and committed to both the mission and each other.

- Do pattern recognition and decisiveness from experience conflate with various biases that actually hinder the feeling of a safe environment?
- Have you slowed down to challenge assumptions and establish expectations ahead of commencing the work?
- Have you thought through how to create an environment that will uplift, elevate, and help people flourish?

CHAPTER 3

# FIRST ENCOUNTER

## *Being Authentic and Vulnerable*

> "I was surprised at how open people were. I think it was the environment. I was shocked at how many people were immediately vulnerable."
>
> —*Al Paxton, Veteran Participant, Ouray, Colorado*

Preparation for the Crucible starts long before anyone shows up at the trailhead, be it in the canyonlands of Utah or the Rocky Mountains of Colorado. Yet, somehow upon arrival, when participants first meet each other in real life, it's often revealed that *preparation* meant something different to each individual. Fred, an executive from the Sunbelt, brought too much food and too many clothes. He was a little embarrassed as he pulled out a different outfit for every day, a "car camping" meal kit, heavy metal water bottles, and even a small axe. Compared to everyone else's lightweight equipment, Fred realized that carrying all the extra weight on his back would certainly slow the team down. A little disheartened, and very embarrassed, he listened to the guides, dumped the nonessential items, and repacked. The pile of clothes and unnecessary gear going back to the car was astonishingly large—like an overfilled laundry basket.

Joe, on the other hand, was a military veteran, and an experienced outdoorsman. He brought a carload of extra gear in case anyone forgot something—an extra sleeping bag, spare trekking poles, and a backup lightweight cooking pot (which Fred happily accepted). Joe could have easily stepped in and taken charge of the gear layout, when the guides explain each piece of gear and its importance, then go over how it should all be packed. For example, food and rain gear go on top, the sleeping bag on the bottom, and no inflatable sleeping pad should be placed on the outside of the pack where it could easily get punctured.

Though Joe's authentic self is to serve, help, support, train, guide, and teach, he realized that "helping" the guides by interrupting them, asserting his expertise and dominance, would have only served himself and his ego. What was best for the team was to defer to the guides. Inspired by Fred's humility, Joe realized he could perhaps learn something from staying quiet, reading the room, and really listening. He followed the guides' lead, even when he thought he knew better on a couple of the tips. In the process, Joe demonstrated a high degree of social intelligence, exhibiting the same ability as Fred to understand the feelings and beliefs of other people and act in a manner that best served the team.

These first encounters have the potential to get off to a rocky start. Participants often posture to set the first impressions they think others want to see instead of acting authentically and showing their true selves. Authenticity comes from vulnerability, because putting yourself out there means not knowing whether you will be accepted by other people. The first encounter can be slow, as participants question whether they truly belong in this new team dynamic.

When a group gets together in person for the first time, they are still strangers, not yet trusted teammates. Some feel they have something to prove and display a "know-it-all attitude," building an emotional wall that shuts others out. A competitive instinct sometimes kicks in, and participants will size each other up. They typically ask, "Is this going to be easier than I thought—or harder? Do I have anything in common with these people, or nothing at all? Which person do I think is going to get my sense of humor?" The bottom-line question right away is: "Did I make the right decision to come here—are these my people?" They're looking for shared values and common goals, and ultimately, they're trying to determine whether these strangers can become friends they can trust.

In these first encounters, trust-building activities can accelerate the development of a high performing team. These interactions allow the team to get to know one another as humans first, coworkers second. Such activities include sharing origin stories, expressing fears and vulnerabilities, showing humility by expressing values and points of view, and admitting what participants don't know or understand. The leaders act as facilitators to ensure equal participation in these discussions. The primary ground rule at this point is that others listen to understand one another and treat each other with dignity and respect.

These discussions are enhanced as some people more easily share their authentic selves, and show vulnerability from the start. It takes courage to be the first to admit you're afraid, not okay, or worried about letting people down. Those are the people who risk saying what they think, speak up if they have valid concerns, and remain curious about other people around them. During a Crucible, participants are reminded that, unlike the environment where they earn their livelihood, no one should have anything to prove, protect, or promote here. Instead, it is not only okay, but expected that they seek support, ask for help, and take a helping hand when offered. As a leader, part of your job is to help your people understand the responsibility to build a better, more authentic, and cooperative team from the get-go. By reframing expectations, solidifying a foundation of trust, and clarifying the common purpose, these first encounters can help everyone open up and begin forming a truly functional, indomitable team from the start.

## ACCEPTANCE VS. ASSUMPTIONS

Do I belong here?

With these people?

In this place?

At this time?

Those are the unasked questions at the start of every expedition. They are the same questions we ask ourselves when we encounter most new groups, whether it's a new project team at work, a new assignment, or a new social club we're joining. We wonder what our common ground is with these strangers, if any, and whether or not they can be trusted. At its most basic, trust is the willingness to be vulnerable with others while knowing they may or may not reciprocate by showing their own vulnerability.

Trust is the foundation of every team—it has been since the days of the earliest humans cooperating to survive. We're tribal. We want to be around people who think like us, believe what we believe, and operate with a similar definition of ethics that governs our behavior. We come together in teams to differentiate ourselves, to earn status, and at a very basic level, to ensure our safety and security. But we also come together to accomplish heroic and audacious goals we couldn't do by ourselves. In short, we come together to be part of something bigger.

Unlike the nearly 360-degree vision of some prey, humans have predator eyes, evolved to face forward. We must trust and rely on others to ensure our modern version of survival and success. So, when we go it alone, we are incredibly vulnerable. With any first encounter, whether consciously or not, we consider our desire for independence against the reality of our need for interdependence. To help develop a feeling of safety from the start, leaders must create an environment in which the team understands the expectation to make deeper connections, seeking to understand one another's values, assumptions, beliefs, and expectations.

Leaders create this safe, communal environment when they help people develop empathy through skills like caring, listening, and asking questions, all of which can be developed and reinforced. But you can't develop a relationship if you don't care, and it's hard to care if you don't know the people around you. You learn who they are by being curious—and as discussed in chapter one, when you're curious, you ask questions. When you listen to the answers, instead of just hearing them, you come to understand the person or people you're speaking to.

The connection formed through this deeper level of listening can be profound. When people receive our undivided attention, they are much more likely to return the favor by showing an interest in what makes us tick. This is the law of reciprocity. The simplest way to make this a maxim for a team is with two words and a greater-than symbol: Give > Take. Sometimes the best direction is the most concise. Asking people to give more than they take will help teammates gain acceptance with one another, and alleviate incorrect assumptions about what people believe, value, and expect.

Just as assumptions cannot be made during the preparation stage, they must be withheld during the first encounter as well. It's important to remember we all make assumptions when we interact with others. The more experience we gain, the faster we're able to spot patterns, identify trends, and make quick decisions. That well-developed acumen can be a strength, but it can also mask biases, which are rooted in what we assume. Assumptions come from what we observe, what we select to home in on, and how we interpret what we're experiencing. The assumptions we make lead to conclusions, hard-to-change beliefs, and ultimately, our actions.

You can imagine what the group was assuming about Fred when they recognized he had packed poorly for the Crucible: He hadn't paid attention to details on the preparation conference calls; he was being selfish because he would need to be taken care of along the journey; and he was not someone who would be reliable or dependable during the trek. The assumptions subconsciously shaped the team's beliefs about him, colored their initial interactions, and influenced how they predicted he'd act in the future. Unfortunately, those assumptions and biases can lead to self-fulfilling prophecies. Since people expected adverse behavior from Fred, that's all they saw, and their response only led to Fred feeling frustrated and becoming despondent.

Without specifically calling out Fred, the team had to be guided to pay attention to their assumptions, seek first to understand, and realize that their biases could lead to dysfunction. In such a situation a leader must instill a focus on the positives and fairness, not judgment. Attention should be given to catching people doing things right as compared to the mistakes they've already made. Research shows that for people to feel they've been treated fairly, positive interactions have to outnumber negative interactions at a ratio of at least five to one.[1] As a leader, you must ask open-ended questions to get people to think before assuming, and acting on those assumptions. These questions can include:

- What are they seeing and interpreting as factual?
- How might they test assumptions while being willing to be proven wrong?
- What would it take to extend grace to those with whom they already formed a negative impression?
- What do those assumptions say about them? Rather than point a finger, can they pull their thumb?
- Are they projecting their own insecurities on others in order to make themselves feel better?

Though we all know the phrase "seeing is believing," more often than not, *believing is seeing*: We look for evidence that confirms our beliefs. We allow our assumptions and biases to take over, causing us to act toward others in ways that reinforce the conclusions we have already formed. The ways leaders facilitate pushing teammates beyond these initial assumptions to help their team remain open and curious allows them to explore the real value each teammate brings, regardless of first impressions.

You must emphasize the absolute necessity of understanding where people are coming from, including what they value, believe, and expect from the experience of collaborating on something bigger than themselves. Encouraging teammates to talk to each member of the team early on regardless of their initial impression of who they think they "fit" best with can be a way to nudge everyone toward uncovering and disproving (or affirming) their assumptions with factual information. Being open and curious in this process will allow teammates to truly listen as opposed to hearing what they expect. The grace given in return, in spite of the first impression they may have made, can be hugely impactful.

Rather than have your team think of how they want to project themselves to the group as they would in a classic work environment, ask them from the start to learn about others in the group. Go around to each team member and discuss the following:

- What do they see as the value of the experience on which they are embarking and how does that line up to their own purpose?
- How do they expect the progress toward the objectives will go? What will be easy and what will be hard?
- What do they personally hope to contribute to others during this experience?

These brief talking points can give context to teammates so they know where to initially begin a conversation and find connection points along the way that serve both the individual and the team. While you may have served in sales, and a team member may have a background in

IT, you both may realize a common connection around what you see as important—that is, what you both truly value.

As an executive and veteran stated during one Crucible, "Leadership doesn't start at the event, it starts before." A team cannot wait until the demands are heavy and the pressure is on. They must get to know one another early, eliminating assumptions and orienting individuals toward connecting. That process can create a team unlike any other, one in which people feel safe to show their authentic selves. By understanding what people are really all about and what they want from any given experience, you can create a team where people feel they belong and who will start to have each other's backs from the first step on the trail.

### Hold Your Views Lightly

Despite the very human desire to be around people "like us," diversity of thought is a major requirement of a high performing team. For diversity to work, it requires us to hold our views lightly. We must be open to being proven wrong and to taking in information that contradicts, or disproves, our long-held assumptions and beliefs. Only then can we gain an understanding of our teammates. This means checking our assumptions and withholding our judgment. Still, habits are hard to break.

For example, Nick was an elite special operations soldier, retiring from the Army after more than twenty years, including multiple combat deployments to places no one would describe as vacation hot spots. As the time for the expedition grew closer, he began realizing he and his fellow veterans were going to have to carry the executives over the course of the journey if everyone was going to arrive unscathed on the other side.

The first challenge was getting to the trailhead, a three-hour drive through snow-covered roads in Colorado. Nick was riding in Beth's car, accompanied by a couple other teammates. Nick started out the drive feeling a bit tense, as Beth, an executive participant from the flatlands of the East Coast, slowly made her way through the snow. He wondered if he might have to step in and take the wheel. But along the sometimes sketchy drive, conversation flowed and everyone started gaining a better sense of each other. By the time they reached the trailhead, Nick realized how easy the trip had been. He told Beth he had been impressed with her driving skills as well as with her ability to remain calm along the route. He was happy she had already proven his initial bias about executives wrong. She appreciated his generosity and laughed—she admitted she had a white-knuckle grip on the steering wheel the whole time!

One of the ways to check whether you are holding your views lightly comes from a concept developed way back in 1936: the original self-help guru, and business philosopher, Dale Carnegie inferred that we should be *interested* versus *interesting*. This was from his seminal book, *How to Win Friends and Influence People*, which is still a bestseller today—for good reason. If we constantly try to make others interested in us, we won't take the time to pause and get to know them. Instead, we'll be dominating conversations, asserting our views, and never giving ourselves the opportunity to learn about others' points of views that could profoundly affect us.

People don't come with an instruction manual. Before civilization six thousand years ago, we only had to keep track of about 150 other people, many of whom were family. If we didn't follow the rules, you can guess what happened. Our world now is more complex than ever with relationships we manage in person, and those we only manage virtually, or asynchronously. It's critical that we seek to understand others if we wish to influence them. And to influence is to understand what others value, what drives them, and what they want. When we help other people get what they want, we get what we want. And hopefully, what you want involves the noble pursuit of a common goal with others.

## AUTHENTICITY AND VULNERABILITY

Acknowledging and discussing your assumptions, biases, and beliefs requires you to be confidently vulnerable, perhaps with people whom you just met. That can be difficult if you aren't quite sure if you can, or should, place your trust in others. But silence hides complacency, malaise, and apathy, and it signals an unsafe environment for debate, dialogue, and authenticity. You must therefore speak up. Vulnerability is like an investment in confidence—you have to give of yourself, open up, and see that the return on opening up is trust from others. As trust grows, you will help create an environment in which your team feels safe enough to be open and authentic and where the best ideas will surface quickly.

As a leader, your willingness to role model your vulnerability allows your teammates to do the same. Vulnerability displays who you really are, a way of sharing your strengths and shortcomings with the team and living in alignment with your values. Leading with values means that others see you exhibit behaviors that align with those values, which is necessary to gain credibility, and to be trusted, reliable, dependable, and predictable. After all, if you're not being authentic, who are you pretending to be?

Revealing more of your authentic self quickly helps create an environment that brings out the best in people. By being authentic in return, your teammates don't have to put up a façade or try to figure out how they "should" be acting in a given situation. Instead, they can just be themselves, allowing them to focus their energy on the team and the tasks ahead.

In the first hour together, we can begin to predict how the Crucible is going to go. If teammates leave their guard up, refusing to share, or give and receive feedback, we have our work cut out for us. But if, instead, they open themselves up through vulnerability, we will see each teammate grow exponentially in our short time together. The group strengthens when they explore their collective blind spots by asking the question, *What are things we don't know we don't know?* The challenges that they will face may be unknowable at this point, but taking the time to explore what else they should be considering, what assumptions they are making, or what they are taking for granted will allow them to get to the root cause of issues, and generate creative options for solutions.

Once shown, vulnerability becomes reciprocal, and it actually helps erase insecurities to strengthen self-confidence. By sharing your authentic self with a sense of humility, you do the rest of the team a service, helping them become more open, willing to ask for help, and supporting each other in return. This sets a tone of camaraderie that will carry throughout any endeavor.

## FINDING STRENGTHS IN OTHERS

On a Crucible in Patagonia, participants spent a week on the third largest ice cap in the world. The weather was, at times, pretty terrible. There was a lot to complain about—biting cold, sore knees, numb extremities, terrifying ledges, and the monotony of walking hours on end, feeling like the destination was never getting any closer. Though no one verbalized their personal suffering, the group had shown a genuine interest in getting to know one another early on, so they became good at picking up on nonverbal cues of pains not spoken. In essence, the team knew each other's strengths and weaknesses more acutely, allowing them to highlight blind spots and recognize veiled façades in one another. It was in these moments of recognition that people offered each other encouraging words, or an aspirin, or an ace bandage. That selflessness, and sense of duty to one another, was the fulcrum for the team's success, and one of the goals was avoiding any significant injury or mishap.

When asked about what they've learned about leadership over the years, successful soldiers, professors, business titans, authors, and politicians all inevitably say the same thing: "It's not about me." That means helping your team see and recognize their strengths, and support each other to fully leverage them. It is not enough that you perform well, but that you are enabling the best in your teammates. After all, it's easy to find fault in people—super easy. What's much harder is to find strengths. But by approaching a group's first encounter with authenticity and vulnerability, and setting aside assumptions and biases, you can find those strengths quickly. This not only helps you better understand the developing team dynamic, but it also allows you to encourage teammates, and set an example so they encourage each other in return. You want people to feel welcomed, and that they will be treated fairly, and then they will naturally open up to the team.

In a professional setting, anything you can do to help people authentically connect as quickly as possible will serve the team well. For example, teammates may use photos representing stories to create simple prompts, such as a personal hero, a crucible experience that shaped them, their family and friends, or something they're proud of. This exercise can allow teammates to find commonalities, increase awareness of each other's journeys, and create more meaningful ways to collaborate.

**PRO TIP**

ABL (always be listening)—and remember you have to be curious to care. Use the Four A's to ensure you remain interested and authentic:

- Ask: Make sure your questions are open-ended.
- Again: Ask again, and clarify your understanding with good follow-up questions.
- Act: Express your intentions, and do what you say you will do.
- Adapt: Did your action produce the desired effect, and what adaptation is needed to improve?

▲▲▲

Now take a moment to consider your own organization and how you approach first encounters:

- In what types of social situations are you most comfortable? What does the environment look like where you can be your authentic self?
- In what conditions are you most willing to give feedback? What would allow you to give feedback sooner to more people?
- What new experiences might help you learn more about yourself? How can you create those opportunities?

## THE REST OF THE STORY

When one teammate displays humility, and acknowledges what they don't know, it changes the tone of the experience for everyone in a positive way. Others are willing to suspend self-protective behaviors to lean into learning and growth, safety and trust. For Fred, the executive who brought too much gear, his takeaway was being prepared is being prepared to be . . . *vulnerable.* That is to say, "I'm not sure what I am doing here, and I need some help figuring out what I actually need for this expedition." Fred has a picture of all the gear we took from his pack that he looks at occasionally to remind him that part of preparation is focus, saying no to things that aren't critical, and asking for assistance.

For Joe, the military veteran, he learned in retrospect that it's very easy for him to assume the role of a trainer. After all, that's what he's always done—that's who he is. But with a new team, and a new dynamic, the best thing for him to do was to sit back and figure out what other unique attributes he could bring to the team other than "being the smartest guy." Not every problem set needs training, and high level leaders know they can't dilute their focus by solving every single problem set. With this mindset, he was able to start using different "muscles" that forced him from his comfort zone, and in the long run, were necessary for his professional growth.

## CONCLUSION

How you use the first encounter to reinforce the values you established in the selection process matters. Don't let the first encounter become simply administrative, but a powerful opportunity to create excitement and buy-in from your team. The first encounter is all about creating an environment for the team to effectively lean in and work together. The willingness to put oneself out there, flaws and all, allows one to lean in hard with nothing to prove, protect, or promote. The reciprocal power of this vulnerability is that others will quickly join you. It's the personal responsibility of each person to risk saying what they think, and it's what the leader must articulate early on as an expectation.

The proof is in the pudding, and the effective leader is intentional, deliberate, articulate, and concise in conveying their expectation for behaviors and results. Two of the key ingredients of performance are the expectation that team members are authentic and vulnerable, and that everyone treats each other with dignity and respect while holding their views lightly. You have to care to listen. You have to listen to hear. You have to hear to feel. And you have to feel to lead.

## THE THREE PILLARS

### *Leading Self*

It's critical to arrive at the first encounter interested in others versus anxious to establish your bona fides. When a team is forming, people are often concerned about their own insecurities and want to ensure that their image and interests are protected, causing them to show up in an inauthentic and, sometimes, selfish way. Getting clarity on what value you bring to the team and what you want to learn from others can help you operate in a more productive manner.

- What do you expect of others?
- What can others expect from you?
- Are you taking the initiative to set aside your agenda and make others feel welcome?

### *Leading Others*

The first engagement is about learning what drives others, and what their expectations are for the collaboration. Defaulting toward interest in others over interest in self will create a culture in which people lean in to support one another.

- What drives each of your teammates?
- What are their goals and aspirations?
- What are their expectations of others?

### *Leading the Organization*

First impressions are lasting, and the expectations set early on are the performance standards required when inevitable obstacles are encountered.

- What does the environment *feel* like to work in?
- Do people assign blame or co-create solutions?
- Do people work with each other, or for each other?

CHAPTER 4

# MOVEMENT

## *Setting Direction, Pace, and Tone*

> "I made early assumptions that if I was fine with the pace, the rest of the group was as well. I made assumptions about how people felt that we never discussed. Being empathetic as a leader, thinking on others' behalf, beyond the direction, is a powerful trait."
>
> —*Terence Bennett, Executive Participant and Veteran, San Juan Mountains, Colorado*

Picture Patagonia. That iconic mountainscape, with Mt. Fitz Roy towering above ancient glaciers and rocky moraine. A twelve-person team is standing on a glacier, the wind whipping across their chapped faces. Team members alternate between uncontrollable shivering in the frigid wind and baking in the glaring sun, sweating profusely as they lug their gear up the glacier, which seems to go on forever. In snowshoes, roped together, and hiking in a trancelike cadence, there is no end in sight. They have over fifty more miles until their destination for the night. The only form of wildlife they've seen in a week has been a single bumblebee buzzing down the line.

Then, one of the veterans on the trek yells, "We're at the PONeR!"

"What did he say?" one of the executives asks.

"We're at the P. O. N. R.—the Point of No Return! It's three days that way—and three days if we turn around. It's too windy for choppers!"

When you get to a P.O.N.R., the stakes become extremely high. On a glacier, if anyone gets sick or injured, evacuation will be arduous, to say the least. That's when it hits the team: whether they retreat or press onward, they can only move as fast as their slowest person. And pace is not the only concern: any forward movement must also account for direction and attitude—what we refer to as the tone of the team. That means getting the direction right, setting a sustainable pace that can be met by all members of the team, and doing so with an intentionality about how people feel along the way.

An expedition is finite—there is a finish line. In the business world, there is no such destination, just new objectives once the quarter ends or a project comes to a close. There's always more to do! A constant, steady forward movement means you need to push your people all the time. But you also need to know how to help them stretch their limits, without breaking them. If they feel that nothing they do is good enough, or if they feel detached from their work, their engagement will be reduced, and their spirit may falter. People can bounce back with resilience when their limits have been tested, but not as easily when they've been broken. This concept applies to physical stamina as much as it does to mental acuity and emotional well-being.

A defined direction, pace, and tone are therefore absolutely necessary to handle the endless goals any organization faces. When leaders get these right, the result is a group of high performing individuals intent on achieving goals and overcoming obstacles as they arise. They're indomitable, and collectively, those individuals form a nearly unstoppable team, one that has an uncommon loyalty and duty to each other that shows up as genuine humility and compassion, commitment, and focused energy. With those team traits, extraordinary results will follow.

Before we explore direction, pace, and tone separately, here is an easy way to think about each concept throughout the chapter:

- **Direction** is about engaging the head. People need to understand where they are going so they can make decisions to support the course ahead.
- **Pace** is about engaging the hands. We use our hands to get work done, and they're how a team gets to where they're going.
- **Tone** is about engaging the heart. Leaders need to be intentional about how they want the team to feel before, during, and after the work, and they do this by helping people find deep purpose and meaning in their role, and the value it provides to others.

In today's dynamic environment, there are many factors outside of a leader's control that have both direct and indirect impacts on individuals, teams, and organizations. These include external issues like inflation, supply chain challenges, recessions, and labor shortages. Instead of focusing energy on trying to control the things you can't, however, you'll find more success focusing on the internal factors you can, which all come down to execution. And execution is a result of your team's direction, pace, and tone (their head, hands, and heart). With that in mind, let's take a deeper look at each, starting with direction.

## DIRECTION

Direction on a Crucible is about getting people from point A to point B, whether that be a base camp or a mountain summit. For organizations, setting direction starts with setting expectations that clearly and concisely define goals, objectives, metrics, and behaviors (as introduced in chapter two). Setting direction can actually be pretty straightforward. We often don't get confused about what we need to accomplish. But putting direction into action is another matter.

Action here requires the integration of the five components of emotional intelligence: self-awareness, motivation, empathy, social skills, and self-regulation. When it comes to setting direction, role modeling self-regulation, or self-discipline, is the pinnacle of these five traits. Self-regulation means displaying confidence, providing inspiration, and creating hope. It also refers to serving the needs of your team given the circumstance. By regulating your emotional response, you can deliver what's best for the team. This is only possible by remaining positive and patient, and not giving in to an outburst that satisfies the need to "be right," which only serves one's pride and ego. This is a tall order, since all humans tend to be emotional creatures who are sometimes rational, versus rational creatures who are sometimes emotional!

During Crucible expeditions, the person who is to lead the movement of the team rotates every day. A critical job for that leader each morning is to brief the team on the plan for the day, explaining how to get from where they are to where they're going. This does not just mean describing the direction of travel, but what will be required at the outset and along the way. Direction for a Crucible typically covers the following:

1. **Departure.** By solidifying the departure time, you allow the team to plan appropriately, ensuring they are on time, ready, and reliable to each other. It's about removing any ambiguities and making things simple, which can only happen when expectations are aligned.
2. **Distance.** The distance to walk (in time and miles) and the elevation gain (in feet) must be understood by the whole team. Without understanding the distance to travel, the team may not

be mentally prepared, nor pack enough food and water to get them through the journey.

3. **Expected Surroundings.** The terrain, in terms of cacti, ice, boulder fields, cliffs, slippery rocks, and the like, must be discussed before it is tackled. Each teammate may need to mentally prepare in different ways depending on the environment and their comfort level. Painting a clear picture of what lies ahead allows teammates to be at their best as they start off. Still, they must recognize they will need to adapt, because every contingency cannot be anticipated.
4. **Breaks.** There's a science here: though participants will definitely need breaks, those moments of rest should not be too long, nor too frequent. Stopping for too long can cause lactic acid to build up, making one's legs feel heavy. Long breaks can also lead to people becoming cold, causing them to spend too much time putting on layers that will likely have to be removed once the team starts moving again. Short breaks, on the other hand, avoid these issues, and most importantly, allow the team to maintain its momentum—a highly motivating factor.
5. **Necessary Gear.** Think of being organized as compressing time. The more efficient each member of the team, the greater momentum they can carry forward. By having the necessary gear accessible when needed (for example, your climbing harness and helmet on the top of the pack), the focus stays on the direction forward, not on searching around in one's bag and causing others to wait.
6. **Water to Carry.** Knowing the proper amount of water to carry, and when to stop to pump water from a stream or puddle, is vital. Water is heavy—too much and it will slow people down and wear them out. Too little can lead to dehydration, causing headaches and muscle cramps. It's a little like Goldilocks getting

things just right. People must make it their personal responsibility to carry the appropriate amount. Still, they often need direction as to how much water will likely be needed.

7. **Accountability Partners.** While self-reliance is necessary to be reliable, we all struggle in different ways, and the accountability partner is there to provide support when the team is under stress. Part of being an effective leader is being a solid follower. Without someone whom you trust in your corner, it can be difficult to display the humility to say, "I don't know, I don't understand, I need help." Creating those relationships between individuals, where they have the trust to be vulnerable, allows for accountability when their self-reliance wavers.

On the Crucible, these seven items are discussed every morning. The following list shows the corollaries for leaders in a business environment. When discussed with regularity, especially when you begin a new effort, these items ensure team alignment:

1. **Deadline.** Team members should be able to rely on each other—and you as their leader—to complete clearly defined tasks by a certain date. A deadline can also be a prerequisite on which future work is dependent. Without meaningful deadlines, it is inevitable that tasks will drag on far too long. Deadlines keep teams focused on providing the best product or service possible in a time frame that creates the most value. Deadlines build trust, and consistently meeting those deadlines is the mark of a well-disciplined team.
2. **Goals.** "Big, Hairy, Audacious Goals," a phrase coined by business author and consultant Jim Collins, are important to keep the organization challenged and moving forward, but they must also be realistic. By setting attainable stretch goals that exceed client expectations, you will uncover strengths in your team and

drive them forward. An aligned purpose with corresponding goals allows teams to develop to their greatest potential.

3. **Expected Issues and Distraction.** Though there are many external issues that are out of your control, you must choose to focus on the internal ones: who is hired, who is promoted, various processes, aligned incentives, and organizational structure. Further, by pressure testing the team's objectives and contingency plans (through pre-mortems, for example, as discussed in the "pro tip" later in the chapter), you can help ensure success.
4. **Breaks.** Unlike machines, we humans have limits to our energy and output, and we cannot work without periods of rest and recuperation. Be clear regarding expectations for what work will be conducted at nights and on weekends, and set the example for what "vacation" actually means. This clarity and "practicing what you preach" ensures your team will give 100 percent when they are working, while also giving themselves the necessary recovery time when they are not.
5. **Top Priority.** Teams often have long "to do" lists that don't adequately take the prioritization of the work into account. Given the pace and demand on teams today, some items need to be deprioritized, or eliminated. A great question to ask when determining what should be a priority is, "For how long will this matter?" If it's not months or years, it's probably not truly a priority.
6. **Fair Share.** What is the proper amount of responsibilities for team members, or for you, to take on? Take on too much, and you will wear yourself out, making you an ineffective member of the team. Carry too little, and you'll lose the respect of your peers. Carrying the right work load and delegating appropriately is a personal responsibility, but also a duty to others.
7. **Accountability Partners.** As discussed in chapter two, teammates should feel a responsibility toward each other and their

overall well-being. They should also develop a habit of creating connections across the team through regular check-ins. Gallup engagement surveys[1] have shown that an important source of satisfaction and commitment on the job is having a "friend at work." Said another way, it's critical to have someone at work whom you trust. This is the person to whom you can vent, and someone who can also tell you to "get on with it." The importance of this one-on-one relationship cannot be understated: it increases the feeling that you matter and belong, because there is someone whom you can count on at all times, someone you trust and who will be there for you when you're down. This person is also someone for whom you would drop everything and do the same.

Leaders on the Crucible rarely get the direction completely perfect right out of the gate. They learn as the days go by, observing how the team works together, and as individuals learn more about their own abilities and needs. As long as they have a learning mindset, they will begin to understand what the team needs and how they can help plan the direction forward. There's an old Army aphorism that was oft cited by General Eisenhower: "Plans are worthless, but planning is everything."[2] The planning allows you to assess risks and prepare for the unexpected. While you can't foresee every possibility, if you have thought deeply about what could happen—and prepared for multiple contingencies—you will be better prepared for the unexpected.

Communicating direction effectively aligns and inspires people, which allows work to happen; encourages commitment from the team, not just compliance; and produces efficiencies that generate the greatest return on energy, time, and treasure. The most effective leaders ensure the direction is understood by all and the goals and objectives are concise. The goals should also be easy to assess, so you can check on their progress and make course corrections along the way. On a Crucible, participants are often asked to identify their location on a map at various times, even if they're not the leader that day. It's critical that everyone pays attention to the route, because even the leader can miss a fork in the road.

Asking, "Where are we?" is a great thing to ask in organizations, too. This question helps everyone see where they are relative to the organization's vision, mission, values, goals, and objectives. It ensures that people understand how their work fits into the big picture. You don't want anyone to think they're just hammering nails; you want them to see the "house" they're building together. The answers to "Where are we?" inform whether your direction has truly been clear, concise, and well understood. If it hasn't, then overall execution is unlikely, and that means missed deadlines, deteriorating quality standards, hits to the morale of your team, and ultimately, a decrease in the satisfaction of your constituents or customers.

## PACE

Getting people up a mountain, or accomplishing any significant aspirational goal, works best when people feel fulfilled, even heroic, about their effort. It's important that the people you work with consistently feel that way, because once you lead them to the summit, you're going to ask them to go down, prepare, and then climb another mountain. To that end, pace is all about sustainability. On a Crucible, that means moving as fast as the slowest person. But it also means clarifying the expected pace per mile to make it to camp well before sunset so you're not setting up in the dark. In an organization, a sustainable pace is one in which you lead your people by managing their energy. Sometimes that may involve working extra hours, but it could also be setting aside downtime to recover from hitting a grueling deadline. The point is to ensure your people don't burn out.

Constant pushing, typical in today's action-addicted business environment, often leads employees toward disengagement and burnout. Though a certain level of stress has actually been shown to enhance performance, once stress overwhelms us, performance declines rapidly, with potential effects on the entire team's goals. Without enough stress, you will stay in your comfort zone and may become complacent. The key is knowing how to ramp up the pressure for yourself and your team so that you can sustain peak performance. When good stress pushes too far and becomes distress, you might crash and burn. Knowing when to add and release pressure is an art that you'll get better at with practice, and that's why it's imperative to know if the pace is stretching versus breaking your team.

You may see this same negative result in your colleagues and friends when they have been pushed to their limit. They become fatigued, don't take pleasure in the things they previously enjoyed, and have a hard time focusing on completing basic tasks. When people feel this level of distress, something has to change for performance and well-being to be achieved. Doing more of the same, or just pushing through, will not improve the outcome.

In short, as discussed in the introduction, we must all learn to slow down to speed up. When we pause, reflect, reconsider, and refocus, we hear what might be otherwise unspoken. It's what authors W. Chan Kim and Renée Mauborgne describe as "feelings uncommunicated, pains unexpressed, and complaints not spoken of."[3] For example, if your team has been working extra hours but you've heard no complaints, you might be deaf to your team's diminishing morale. Most employees are unlikely to approach their boss about this type of issue, in fear of retribution or simply looking weak or unprofessional. It is therefore on you to recognize what's going on with the people around you. Those feelings, pains, and complaints give insight into how we as leaders can better support and encourage our teams.

From a place of understanding, the leader can develop a truly sustainable pace that, despite difficulties, setbacks, and obstacles, people can and will follow. Consider the two-and-a-half-year journey of the 1804–1806 Lewis & Clark Corps of Discovery Expedition. Or the Ernest Shackleton feat of endurance during the Imperial Trans-Antarctic Expedition in 1914–1917. Or NASA's Apollo 13 near-disaster moon mission from April 11 to April 17, 1970. In all three of those crucibles, spanning different times in history, the commonality was what pulled the team through: calm, cool, competent, and collected leaders who knew when to push, when to rest, and when to step back and reflect.

Despite all odds, they got people to do things they otherwise wouldn't do . . . willingly. Can you imagine surviving the western frontier for nearly three years with no outside communication? Or making it through brutal Antarctic winters with diminishing supplies? Or powering down a major system on your spacecraft, which was vital to your reentry to earth—all while floating in a tin can in space? Against all odds, all three teams were so effectively led, they persevered, survived, and even thrived despite severe adversity and less than ideal communication with higher-ups.

On a Crucible, rotating the leaders each day gives each participant an opportunity to test their skills in an austere environment. More importantly, it's a chance for the other members of the team to see how their fellow leaders are deliberate about pace. Do they communicate concisely? Make transparent decisions? Explain a common purpose? When all taken together, does their approach build trust among the team members?

During a trek, participants in the leadership role at the front of the pack tend to set a pace that's too fast—even for themselves. Often, their lack of communication is because they themselves are out of breath. They're laser-focused on "getting there," and they want to prove their drive, strength, and endurance to the rest of the team. Many of these leaders only realize the pace is brutal when they notice the people behind them have stopped talking, and they turn around to find the team is completely spread out to where communication is challenging, if not impossible. People aren't following and thriving—they're simply gasping to catch their breath!

On an expedition in the Rocky Mountains, the objective was to ascend a 13,000-foot peak. Though this may have been daunting in itself, there was a time crunch as well due to looming thunderstorms. The tree line in Colorado is 11,500 feet. Generally speaking, that means you have to get to the summit and back down below the tree line at 11,500 feet before noon, when lightning storms form during the summer months. Halfway through this particular trek, the participants were feeling spent; some were even experiencing a little altitude sickness, including nausea and headaches. The team wanted everyone to safely reach the summit and get down below the tree line before the storm, so they were pushing themselves just a little too hard. The pace was not sustainable but they were so focused on the goal that they weren't paying attention to themselves, let alone their teammates.

One person on the trip became exhausted and hit a physical and mental wall. That exhaustion manifested itself in what appeared to be a panic attack, as they began hyperventilating and crying. The team paused, trying to find good footing on the steep slope and slowing down to assess the situation, including their preparedness and capability. As the cold set in, many started putting on layers. Most were concerned, and everyone felt a little helpless. Those members closest to the person suffering the panic attack helped them regain their composure by letting them know that the feelings they were having were okay. They also provided positive affirmations: "You're almost there. You've done amazing so far. Your family would be so proud of you."

Being the "weakest link" at this stage can have a lasting impact on any teammate for the rest of the journey. The teammate who feels this way may end up carrying this "identity" over the course of the expedition, to create a narrative in their minds that they can't add value to the team. If they get that negative emotion stuck in their head, they can easily drag the whole team down, unless someone finds a way to help them see their unique value.

Many teams can be blinded by "summit fever," the belief that the top priority and most important goal is to make it to the summit of the mountain and back down again. But in this case, the team believed, and rightly so, that safety and everyone's well-being was the top priority and number one goal—not getting to the peak. That meant they wouldn't leave anyone behind, sitting in one spot and waiting as the rest of the group completed the summit. Dividing to conquer was absolutely not an option. And luckily, they didn't have to. Because they were forced to pause, reset, suit up, and rally. The team did summit, and though it was an individual achievement for each person, the fact that the team got there together was an even more meaningful collective accomplishment.

Just like in the business world, it is not simply about moving forward quickly; it's about setting a pace that others can and do willingly follow. Brute force like command and control will only get you so far, and it's no way to inspire the people around you to endure struggles, challenges, setbacks, and strife. Don't confuse activity with results, and busyness with accomplishment, or rush in an effort to "move forward." Busyness may use energy, but that doesn't mean that energy will actually contribute to results. You can't go ninety miles per hour every day. Some days are fast, some are slow, and on some, the team just needs a rest.

## TONE

High level leaders often approach us prior to a retreat or strategic session with their team because they want to practice their latest "pitch" for commitment and action, or how to communicate their vision or strategic plan, and receive our feedback. After hearing the pitch, our typical response is, "Yep, great direction—a stretch, but realistic and doable." But then we ask, "So, how do you want the team to *feel* after you've left the room?"

A furrowed brow comes with the rapid reply, "What? What do you mean, 'How do I want them to *feel*?'"

"Don't you want people to feel elevated and optimistic," we ask, "and that they will actually flourish from the challenge you are setting forth with your call to action?" As you can imagine, this is how they want their teams to feel, even if they don't consider themselves a motivational speaker. They want to have inspired their team to action, not to just have given a vision that they now have to cajole people toward. What we're talking about here is tone—an intentional and deliberate approach to how we want people to feel when guided by our leadership.

At the start of any process, change, or journey, it is inevitable that the team will have a slew of questions, many of which go unasked. How leaders engage with the team to elicit and respond to questions from the beginning sends a clear message about the tone: that it is actually safe to ask the question we feel we should already know the answer to.

On one trip, a senior executive from a major manufacturing organization said, "Before we started, I asked the guides to see the map, what the route was, what our timing should be, and how rough the path was ahead. The guides seemed a little annoyed, as if I was questioning their skills and ability to lead us, but a team got lost the day before and had to go so much further. I spent the time up front to know the game plan so that I could set the team's expectations and I knew that I would be able to confidently lead the team. I went over the plan again in the morning with the team and the team wanted shorter segments between breaks. We conferred over the plan and people agreed."

This proactive approach is ideal, but unfortunately, there is a 100 percent predictable problem for the designated leader on the first day of the Crucible: They will never be able to communicate enough so that everyone around them knows what's going on the entire time. Even if the leaders check in with the team every hour for ten-minute breaks, there will still be unknowns. The following questions often arise:

- Is it okay to tend to my blisters now or should I wait?
- Should I filter more water now, or during the next break?
- How far is it until we get to our destination?
- Is it going to rain before we get there?
- Will we have moonlight tonight in case we get to camp after dark?

Imagine the uncertainty of a team during a major corporate reorganization. There will, hopefully, be scripted big-picture communications that will let your teammates know what is happening, but you will never be able to address every concern or question. Some questions that we see emerge for people are:

- What does my career path look like now?
- How are my responsibilities going to change?
- What can I expect from my new leader?
- Can I work where and when I want?

Creating space for your teams to develop and ask their questions, no matter how insignificant they may seem, will breed a tone of belonging, ownership, and empowerment. The amount of mental and emotional energy invested in these "small" concerns is profound, and if not addressed, they will result in significant productivity loss.

One powerful way to help teams develop and voice their questions is through the practice of "Question Storming." Similar to brainstorming, you want your teams to come into the session open-minded and curious. The obvious questions will emerge first, but don't stop there. Keep developing open-ended questions until you have a flip chart full of questions. This will allow you to really see what you know, and what you don't know, find areas for further exploration, and discover where you need to spend more time investing in relationships and communication to ensure the tone you want is the tone you create.

## ROPED UP

The outcome of setting the right direction, pace, and tone for your team is the interconnected feeling of being "roped up." On the glaciers, being roped up means that four to six people are tethered together with a single rope connecting each of them with a harness around their waist. Being roped up is for safety. If the leader were to accidentally step into a crevasse, the others behind would be a counterbalance to pull that person up and out. Being "roped up" demonstrates the importance of a clearly defined direction, a common purpose, and well-defined roles and responsibilities. It also highlights the need for individual accountability where all team members understand what it means to "stay in your lane," and the judgment to go above and beyond as a sense of duty to one another.

Being roped up forces everyone to walk at exactly the same pace. If you move too fast, you will step on the rope with sharp crampon teeth attached to the bottom of your boot, compromising the rope's integrity, which needs to be well maintained in case of an emergency. On the other hand, if one person walks too slowly, they're going to tug on the waist of the person in front of them. And keep in mind, everyone is walking for eight to ten hours per day carrying fifty pounds or more.

Ultimately, tone is going to drive the motivation of the roped-up team. If there is friction between a couple of teammates, or a need to prove expertise, you see tension in the line. When you are roped up for multiple hours on end, issues need to be resolved, collegiality needs to be maintained, and empathy needs to be freely expressed. If you misstep and pull on the team, grace and the assumption of positive intent will go a long way toward ensuring that you keep your head in the game for the rest of the journey. If, however, there is tension and bickering along the journey, you may arrive at the destination, but the group will likely no longer resemble a "team."

Without the elements of direction, pace, and tone being clearly defined, there will be friction and confusion along the rope. Team members are likely to start thinking:

- *Where the heck is that guy in front going?*
- *Why is the person behind me so slow?*
- *Why so fast?*
- *I lost the map. Has anybody seen it?*
- *I'm sick of staring at the guy in front of me. I travel all this way and all I get is a sunburn and a view of his pack.*
- *I could make better time on my own.*
- *Why do we even need to rope up? It's doubtful there are real dangers ahead.*

Similar thoughts tend to pop up in the work environment:

- *Why don't we go in a different direction?*
- *Seems like I'm having to drag the rest of the group and carry more than my fair share!*
- *Don't they know I'm dealing with a lot of stuff here, not to mention at home?*
- *Where is the responsibility and accountability of the other people on my team?*
- *The tasks for this job are repetitive and mundane—where is the fun in all this?*
- *I don't know why we even call this a team. I could do this way faster if I didn't have to collaborate all the time.*
- *We take way too long to make decisions!*

Despite these concerns, what is remarkable is that when people are roped up, the result is a tremendous amount of empathy, kindness, and selflessness, because everyone will struggle and suffer at different times. But there is also a sort of respectful challenging among the people on the rope: "Come on, I know you can dig deep!" And there is realistic optimism: "This is going to suck, but we'll get through it."

In most organizations, an interdependency exists between teams and departments. Our success is, in essence, "roped up" to each other's success. How we ensure we're all moving in the same direction at mutually supportive pacing, and making sure hope and optimism reign, is critical to the success of the overall objectives.

There are certainly times when teams agree to a specific direction, but once they walk out of the meeting, they do their own thing. They assume operations knows better than finance, or sales knows better than marketing. But if the team is moving in different directions for eight to ten hours a day, it won't take long for everyone to get way off course. Even if they are truly aligned on the direction, if one department takes too long to plan and execute their piece, they create strain on others who may have to work in overdrive to achieve the organization's end goal. It might mean the customer leads that marketing generated get ignored by the sales team, or finance misses deadlines preventing an accurate forecast for operations.

If codependent teams can slow down enough to accept the brutal reality of tight deadlines they face and maintain optimism in spite of it, they just may have the capacity to build trust and empathy for each other as the overall tone of the culture. Being "roped up" will allow the team to support one another and accomplish more than might have been otherwise possible.

While being roped up, positivity must be maintained so that when the expected unexpected happens, the team embraces the challenge together with grit, hope, optimism, perseverance, resilience, and resolve.

That's because the leader was intentional about direction, pace, and tone. As we remind people before going on a Crucible, "If you want to go fast, go alone. If you want to go far, we have to go together."

**PRO TIP**

Consider conducting pre-mortems with your team ahead of major initiatives. Effective teams have a cadence of conducting pre-mortems ahead of major projects. Ask, "If this initiative were to fail, why would it? What will have happened?" These questions allow the team to consider a wide range of factors and vulnerabilities that could impact success. Conducting a pre-mortem will ensure you are as prepared as possible, because you will have planned for multiple contingencies.

▲▲▲

Now take a moment to consider your own organization and how you approach setting the direction, establishing the pace, and creating the tone:

- How can you ensure your expectations are well understood?
- What are the questions you ask to determine if the pace of work is sustainable?
- What do you want people to say about working for you and your organization?

## THE REST OF THE STORY

In Patagonia, when the team hit the P.O.N.R. on the third largest ice cap in the world on the border of Argentina and Chile, they pondered next steps. Which direction—push forward or turn around? It hit them like a brick: moving forward might be difficult, but together, sharing this common purpose, it seemed preordained they would forge ahead. And it was unanimous. They moved onward with resolve and positivity. The pace would be set by the slowest person up front leading the way. By individually and collectively pushing themselves to the limit, they achieved their goal of a sixty-mile circumnavigation of Patagonia's Mt. Fitz Roy and Cerro Torre . . . safely, together, and with indomitable will!

## CONCLUSION

The objective is not the only thing that matters on the side of a mountain, or in a business environment. We may reach our goal for the quarter, but by laying off thousands of people, it puts a severe dent in our reputation and our ability to have engaged teams deliver in the following quarter, and beyond. Getting clear in your vision and setting a direction to achieve is the first step to accomplishing any team's mission, but it is not enough. The behaviors and feelings of the team matter. When leaders take the time to effectively define, communicate, and model the pace they expect of their teammates and consider the impact on teams and families, they create not only a sustainable environment, but one where people feel valued and have a gratitude of privilege that they are part of something big, important, and noble.

## THE THREE PILLARS

### *Leading Self*

You cannot go ninety miles per hour for an extended period of time. Before you can set a pace for your team, you have to set a sustainable pace for yourself that allows you to be reliable for others.

- How are you really doing—can you maintain the current pace?
- What can you do to positively impact the current situation by setting an example?
- Is the work properly structured to maximize and balance your quality of performance with the efficiency of your work?

### *Leading Others*

With alignment, communication is key. Think twice about whether the assumption that a weekly fifteen-minute stand-up meeting will be enough communication for a complex project. Take the time to ensure your team is committed to the goal and feel positive about their purpose.

- What do you do to create an environment where people will provide honest feedback?
- What are the best metrics to determine whether you have real commitment—not just compliance?
- How can you best support your team?

### *Leading the Organization*

Performance is ultimately about where you are going—the direction. It is up to the leader to chart the course by setting realistic goals and objectives with key metrics. If people don't know where they are going, they cannot develop a sustainable pace or engage meaningfully with the work.

- Is the team aligned on the direction, and have they had an opportunity to voice concerns, suggestions, and ideas?
- Are deadlines and goal dependencies outlined clearly and concisely so the team knows "who does what by when" for all goals and objectives?
- Have you gone beyond defining where you are going to help establish the "why" so the team can become fully committed?

CHAPTER 5

# BASE CAMP

## *Reenergizing and Reengaging*

> "At base camp, we all set about doing the immediate tasks needed to take care of ourselves first. Water filtering was an informal gathering point, like the community well. These moments allowed us to connect early on, and productively, while rebuilding energy at our own pace."
>
> —*Jason Field, Executive Participant, Ouray, Colorado*

After a long day trekking up the side of a glacier, the team in Patagonia reached the spot where they would make camp for the night. On the edge of the mountain range, the ground couldn't really be called "ground" at all. Rocks and boulders, the smallest the size of bowling balls, covered every inch beneath their feet. Though hard to walk on, they came in handy: the team used the rocks to create two-foot walls on the windward side of each tent, blocking the wind just enough so they could attempt to erect their tents. Gathering and placing the rocks to form a windshield took the better part of an hour.

Individually setting up a tent in this wind would be impossible, so the team partnered up. Each pair had to hold on to that tent for dear life, because if the wind took hold, it would have been in Antarctica before long, and they'd be in dire straits with no shelter. Adding to the misery was sixty-mile-per-hour sustained winds, and a temperature below freezing, making the windchill below zero. In such an environment, you can't hear anyone speaking, and your fingers don't do what you want them to. And, of course, the two requirements to pitching a tent are communication and dexterity!

In the fierce, relentless gusts, Doug—a veteran with experience in extreme environments all over the world—decided the best way to prevent the tent from blowing away was to climb in while his partner, Jared, used boulders to hold the tent down. Jared placed two boulders on the windward corners of the tent closest to the small wall the team had built. He brushed the dirt off his gloves, looking at a job well done. But then he heard some sort of hollering scream coming from Doug. With the wind blasting his face, Jared adjusted the hood of his jacket, squinted his eyes, and looked up. The tent was now two feet off the ground—with Doug inside. A surreal scene ensued. Jared peered into the tent's opening and saw Doug on what could only be described as a magic carpet ride. The wind was that strong, and Doug was not that light!

Despite the miserable conditions, the moment provided a glint of humor, along with the motivation to get that tent onto and into the ground so they would be set for the night and could get some food in their bellies. They knew they had a long, cold, dark night ahead, and attempting to sleep in gale-force winds relentlessly slapping every inch of their tent's fabric would be difficult. But they were relieved to have made it to base camp.

A base camp is a place where camaraderie is fostered, trust grows, and a feeling of belonging sets in. It culminates in a collective sense of duty to one another. It is where wounds are tended, apologies made, and the events of the day are reviewed through different lenses. Each team member has a responsibility to honestly assess what's worked, what hasn't, and what changes are needed in the following days. Base camp also provides the opportunity for rest, reflection, and yes, preparation once again for the day ahead, based on the wisdom gained from what was learned the day before.

The base camp is not just a physical place, but a mental one—a safe space where people feel they matter and belong. It's a place where people learn to be more self-reliant so they can be reliable to each other. And it's an environment in which the goal is to solidify and reinforce a common purpose and sense of trust. When done well, it's a place where no one wants to let anyone else down.

Getting to base camp might feel like the finish line, but it's just another starting point, a place to reenergize and reengage. When you are dog-tired, the hardest part of the day may occur when you think you can finally rest; but then you have to find another gear to do what must be done before nightfall, instead of putting it off until tomorrow. Helping people find that other gear is part of what defines leadership, allowing them to see their obligation in the service of the team as a deep commitment. It's about role modeling fortitude and expecting resilience.

## CULTIVATING AN EFFECTIVE BASE CAMP

Though base camp is all about reenergizing and reengaging, when a team gets to base camp, there's still a lot to do before they can rest. Critical tasks must be undertaken, all of which differ based on the situation. Still, certain tasks are always a priority. For the Crucible, it's up to the leader to provide clarity with regard to task prioritization in four main areas:

- **Shelter.** Participants must get their tents set up on a piece of flat ground away from any tree limbs that might fall. Flat ground is important for watershed and comfort. Even a slight incline can make for a long, restless night—or a waterlogged tent if there's even a little bit of rain. Ideally, the shelter is established in dry weather before nightfall. If it's raining or dark, the task becomes a whole different sort of challenge. This is where the leader can see a team operating selflessly to help each other, or individuals struggling alone. It takes sacrifice to delay setting up your warm and cozy little spot to help others, but that sort of sacrifice is what distinguishes a high performing team from others.

- **Hygiene and Health.** Each team member's hygiene and health are their own responsibility. If they don't take care of themselves, they certainly can't take care of each other. The same goes for you as their leader. Consider your feet. On an outdoor expedition, your feet are your wheels. Without them working at 100 percent, you're in for a potential disaster. You must change your socks as needed and address any hot spots or blisters as they form. This is a perfect example of self-reliance—it's not up to others to carry a blister kit for you, and if your blisters prevent you from hiking, you're an automatic liability to the team, and the team's mission.
- **Water.** At base camp, it's necessary to locate a clean water source, and fill up at night before the water freezes over. Extra water is needed for cooking, but also for miscellaneous uses, like filling a bottle with hot water and placing it in your sleeping bag for a little extra warmth. Often, a small team will volunteer to get water for everyone to expedite the scouting and gathering and make the workload more efficient.
- **Food.** Everyone on the team needs to know how to safely operate the portable stoves. If they're not careful, accidents happen, whether when boiling water to hydrate a freeze-dried meal or preparing some coffee the following morning. If someone gets

> burned or food is destroyed, the mission can be fundamentally changed. Even though this might seem minor, when on an expedition, you don't want any injuries getting in the way of forward progress, and food is precious—it's energy needed to accomplish the goal at hand.

When this hierarchy of needs is addressed, individuals and the team as a whole can finally rest, which is necessary to properly and fully reenergize. Though they may be thinking about the challenges ahead, and checking all their to-dos off their lists, they realize they need to free up the space to relish the quiet, focus on what truly matters, and let their guard down to be vulnerable, relax, and appreciate the moment.

When we get overwhelmed with all the undone tasks, it's nearly impossible to focus on the now, or prepare for what comes next—or even decide what *should* come next. We become disengaged, focusing on our own internal issues and thinking less of the group and experience around us. A constantly racing mind keeps us up at night, takes us out of the moment, and doesn't jibe with the restorative nature of rest we all need at the end of a hard day or project.

Imagine when you have left work undone and you know you need to send an email in the morning, or you have something important for which you'll need to wake up early. Your sleep is inevitably disrupted as you obsessively check the clock every few minutes, wondering if you have overslept. Taking care of the important tasks first truly does create the space for ourselves and our teams to restore energy, renew passion, and reignite what drives us. We cannot continue to push toward goals without reenergizing through effective rest.

These four areas of concern at a physical base camp—shelter, hygiene and health, water, and food—correlate with four areas of concern you are likely to experience as a leader in a work setting at your everyday "base camp." They start with "culture."

### *Culture*

Culture is a lot like shelter. Your workplace must be one in which trust is built on a commitment to transparency, authenticity, and reliability, and where teammates feel safe enough to risk saying what they think. This shelter is of course safe in terms of a physically comfortable, inviting workspace, but more importantly, it's a mental and social shelter as well. As touched upon in the introduction, such a positive environment does not just come about by chance—it must be intentional.

Leaders who create a great culture are those who think more like *designers* than *doers*. To get the culture right, you have to think like a designer with consideration to four levers:

**People – Structure – Processes – Incentives**

First, *people* are at the heart of the levers. What makes all the difference is that you—the leader—uphold the values and standards of the organization. That means performance is praised, and nonperformance is coached. Praise and recognition propel individuals and teams to high levels of commitment and engagement. By offering ongoing growth and development opportunities, you also help others develop more self-confidence.

What you stand for and support sends a signal to everyone on the team that the values being upheld are equivalent to "doing what you say." Further, role modeling lays the foundation for trust, which is the best retention tool you have. The topic of trust comes up with our clients more than any other challenge. In the bestselling classic *The Five Dysfunctions of a Team: A Leadership Fable*, Patrick Lencioni posits that trust is the foundation upon which healthy conflict, accountability, commitment, and results are built. It's hard to come by, and easy to lose, but when it's strong, trust works like a relationship epoxy. Part of trust is authentic, two-way communication where what is said (and expected) is what was heard (and delivered).

People also want trust in the form of:

- Predictability
- Reliability
- Responsiveness
- Curiosity
- Authenticity
- Selflessness

These attributes can't be easily measured, and they matter for more than just employee retention; they help a team come together and achieve organizational objectives while thriving. The attributes require an investment in really getting to know people as humans, not just cogs and coworkers.

When you have these human capital intangibles, you have a team that demonstrates grit, shows a sense of duty to one another, aligns their focus, and is unbound with a spirit of audacity to do things that didn't seem possible. Retention is as simple and as hard as that. Connecting with your team means making time to form real relationships, and breaking our addiction to *busy*.

You also demonstrate the importance of your people by seeking their feedback for continuous improvement. This not only showcases your graciousness and humility, but it allows you to better lead your team in real time instead of having to stop and reassess every potential issue. By actively listening to your people, you help them feel they belong.

The second lever, and the one most frequently pulled, is *structure*. There is no reason you need to have a hierarchical, command and control structure circa 1990. As seen in the special operations community, "dynamic subordination" can be an effective way to organize a high performing team. In such a structure, the leader defers to others on the team based on the circumstance, the time, the situation, and others' expertise—including their need to take on responsibility to help with their development. You'd be hard pressed to figure out who the actual leader is under dynamic subordination, because you'd be observing fluidity and flow as the team navigates various issues, challenges, problems, and opportunities. Ultimately, this means the leader willingly gives up control, which is an outstanding demonstration of two-way trust.

This approach is often seen on the Crucible when teammates who have more experience in an area give up control to an assigned leader for a given task. Even in the base camp, someone is in charge to help ensure that the collective tasks, such as meal preparation, are done efficiently. Effective leaders in business do the same when they recognize that while they hold the title, and formal authority, of "leader" in a given situation, they are not always best positioned to know, influence, or decide. In response, they allow a direct report or other teammate to lead the team.

The structure lever is most often pulled because of a control mindset inherent in so many leaders. This mindset causes leaders to believe that the problems facing the organization can be fixed by simply shifting responsibility to certain individuals. This approach creates a lot of change and uncertainty, and many leaders don't give the new structure enough time to evolve into a high performing team. As a result, the cycle repeats: another reorganization, more change, additional uncertainty, and never-ending chaos. Instead, structure should boil down to stepping back and thinking like a good physician, making sure you have the right diagnosis before deciding on the most appropriate treatment. Otherwise, poor design decisions can have unintended, deleterious effects.

The third lever is *processes*, which are decision rules for expedient and routine decision-making. Processes also clarify situations that are not routine, those that require a more thoughtful decision-making approach, and allow us to remain efficient despite obstacles. To that end, it must be specified who has decision-making authority and what the prioritized criteria are for making decisions, the best of which should align with stated core values. By creating efficiency, processes can also help an organization scale. At base camp, processes that need to be decided on include how fires will be kept going throughout the night, when the team will come together in the evening, and how the group will operate throughout the morning so they depart on time, which is always critical given the weather.

The fourth lever is *incentives*. That word probably makes you think "money," but we're not talking about compensation at all. Non-monetary incentives can take many forms, from giving teammates the ability to work on meaningful work outside their core responsibilities to finding ways to enhance the team through meaningful opportunities for connection. Incentives have to do with two fundamental responsibilities of the leader. First, you have to make people feel they matter—that their work matters, and they matter as a human being. Second, you have to make people feel they belong. If there is even a whiff of an "old boys' club," it will alienate people. Humans are social animals, and we need to feel we're part of something bigger than ourselves. When you get incentives that drive behavior right (what gets praised versus what gets punished), people feel included and know you genuinely care about them. That's when your people will go through brick walls for each other. Having each other's backs, or a duty to each other, is the ultimate sign of a highly functional team.

Incentives also help people think heroically about their aspirations. By upholding high standards and rewarding success, people are more likely to rise to the level of lofty expectations. A study published in the *Journal of Experimental Psychology* reported that performance can go up a full 40 percent by a leader simply saying to a team member, "I have very high expectations, and I know that you can reach them."[1] Think about that for a moment: one phrase, which simply exhibits a belief in others, can radically improve performance. And why wouldn't you believe in your people? After all, you saw something in them when you selected them to join your team in the first place.

By creating a safe environment where you place trust in people to take responsibility, you receive trust in return, or the benefit of the doubt, when making decisions and providing direction. This environment and culture instills belief. When people know they are cared for, recognize they're part of the team, and understand the high expectations that have been placed on them, they'll be inspired. All of the culture, structure, process, and incentives you've built will help lead to a team that supports each other even in the most difficult journeys—no matter what.

## *Self-Awareness*

Do you know how your proclivities and outward behavior affect other people? And do you have the ability to self-regulate your emotional response by stepping away for a moment to deliver what's best for the team, not what satisfies your own vanity? Self-awareness causes you to recognize that it's not enough for you to be "squared away"; you must possess a sense of duty to be selfless, with no expectation of anything in return, because the goal is to make other people's jobs and lives easier.

Each Crucible Expedition has its unique challenges with weather, terrain, and group dynamics, but one base camp that stands out was in the Rocky Mountains. As one participant recalled, "We were told to spread out and choose the location for our tents. I was thinking we needed to get everything done before we ran out of daylight. We had most of everything we needed except water, so if you got set up before everyone else, getting water for everyone was an unspoken expectation. There was a dichotomy of a need to be self-reliant, to be able to take care of yourself so that others did not have to take care of you, while also recognizing that when I am in a position to help teammates out, I can and should." That type of self-awareness creates a group effort and a willingness to support one another.

In business, such self-awareness manifests itself as teammates helping to move the team forward with little consideration for their own recognition or credit. Leaders sometimes struggle with selflessness, because part of moving up the ladder at work includes being savvy about promoting oneself and one's team. But when leaders are more focused on ensuring they are recognized as the reason for the success of an initiative than amplifying the success of their teammates, they lose the trust of both their direct reports and, at times, their leaders. As President Harry Truman famously said, "It's amazing what you can accomplish when you do not care who gets the credit." And we know—easier said than done.

### *Clients and Customers*

Water can be scarce, and precious—a lot like the clients or customers that are the reason any business exists. It's easy to be internally focused, but water is life, and clients and customers are the life of a business. A company we worked with affirmed that providing high quality solutions to each of their existing clients was the lifeblood of their business. If they served them well, they thought, clients would come without effort. Their Net Promoter Score—a measure of customer satisfaction based largely on whether a customer would refer the business to others—was off the charts because they had incredibly satisfied customers. Yet, their Net Promoter Score did not positively impact their pipeline. They missed a key insight: in order to grow the business, you must constantly hunt for new clients. This isn't just for your personal success; it's because you owe it to your teammates, your current clients, and any other stakeholders to sustain the business.

Another company we worked for clearly understood the importance of maintaining a steady stream of potential clients and focused on sales. The amount of conflict this created internally almost brought the company to its knees—the delivery teams could not keep up with the constant barrage of new clients, and customers were far from happy. Expectations and incentives were misaligned. The sales team was told to crush it, which they did. Yet they weren't effectively communicating the sales forecast, which meant delivery and production couldn't anticipate the demand through staffing and other efficiency measures needed to scale.

### *Energy*

Food is energy, and its consumption is best when communal. How energy is generated, transferred, regenerated, or lost at your organization is crucial for all of the factors mentioned above. All of us flourish in the presence of light, or positive energy. Known as the heliotropic effect, this is why, for example, plants grow toward the sun. It's also why we look to the light and those people who provide us with energy rather than drain our spirit.

According to research from Professor Kim Cameron at the University of Michigan, the most important factor that accounts for leader and team success is the positive energy of the leader.[2] Energy is more important than strategy, processes, incentives, or even culture. And that positivity translates to higher productivity, quality, morale, customer satisfaction, and financial strength. Recall the law of conservation of energy—energy is neither created nor destroyed. You have to transform your kinetic energy to the potential energy of your entire team. Positivity must be constantly role modeled, and it must be authentic, because people will instantly know if you don't believe what you're saying.

The common thread of effective teams and organizations is the energy level their leaders generate. That energy is a reflection of a capacity and capability to support their people's work and, therefore, results.

As a leader, you have to operate with a marathoner versus sprinter mentality—the long view. You do this by investing in, and developing, the capabilities of your team to meet the capacity demands. And no team is capable of sustaining a grueling pace day after day.

With an awareness of the team's capabilities, the energized leader knows how to set an adaptive pace that gets the team to where they need to be. When the leader increases individual capabilities, the team's capacity expands, and the result is efficiency and scale. Ultimately, as a leader, you have to help people realize they can do more than they thought they could. Reenergizing your team is all about using the concept of positivity to generate energy for yourself, and influencing others with your genuine hope and optimism.

Of course, even all the positive energy in the world doesn't mean you'll be free of obstacles and issues. But that's no cause for alarm: wisdom comes from the inevitable (and expected) failures, setbacks, problems, and mistakes. When you help people develop grit and resilience from their struggles, you transform their attitude, confidence, and drive. And sometimes they find deeper purpose and meaning in their role. Adversity is a reminder that the difficulties we endure today prepare us for tomorrow's inevitable quandary.

As leaders, it's easy to think you have to be singularly great, but the goal is to be remarkably great . . . together. By cultivating collective energy from the people expending the effort, or the work, you create a generator effect that fuels the team and prepares its members for whatever lies ahead.

## BASE CAMP CAMARADERIE

It started to sprinkle. "Tolerable." Then a steady rain. "It's okay—I was prepared for this." By the time they got to base camp in the alpine mountains of Colorado, it was pouring. "Why am I here again?"

As the sun set behind the mountains, it instantly got dark and cold. Soaked to the bone, team members started shivering. Numb fingertips took on that pruned, waterlogged look. Their feet were even worse. Ugh. Waterproof gear was put to the test, and more than one person murmured how all gear should be labeled "water resistant at best"! The last thing anyone wanted to do was gather firewood to even attempt starting a fire. They just wanted to get their tents set up, try to create a clothesline in their cramped quarters to dry out their clothes, and then curl up in a dry-ish, warm-ish sleeping bag.

Yet there they were. A half dozen teammates gathering wood from up to half a mile away and dragging huge logs over undulating terrain. With dark coats, low light, and hoods covering their faces, it was hard to see who was who. In the middle of the stacked wood, in a large ring of fire, crouched the CEO of the team. Not the CEO of the expedition, but the actual CEO of the intact team he signed up for this little foray into the wilderness. In his camouflage hunting jacket, he was using bug spray and a lighter to create a flamethrower to ignite the wet wood. Somehow, he safely got a fire going, slowly backed out, and watched as the bonfire took off, burning bright enough to signal the space station.

Funny thing: a whole bunch of other people then showed up to help with the fire. Only then did the CEO leave to set up his own tent. He took care of his team before he took care of himself. It's easy to say this is part and parcel of being a leader, but it's a whole different story when you're exhausted and feel like all you want to do is collapse. This is when you see what people are made of—their character. The CEO didn't start the fire because he was trying to make a point, or to be a martyr, or to intentionally set an example. He did it because he cares deeply for his team. More to the point, he actually loves his people.

He routinely asks a lot of them, and when he can, he does everything possible to reciprocate by clearing obstacles and providing resources. In this case, it was as simple as fire and its real effect—warmth and security.

But even more than warmth, he changed the environment and created a space where his team could, and did, have breakthrough conversations around that fire later that evening.

The conversation that night started with an outpouring of gratitude for the CEO and others who had helped him. They talked about the day, and how they ended up moving at the speed of the slowest person. Sure, it would have been nice to have gotten to camp before dark, and before the rain. But no one made the slowest person feel bad. In fact, they recognized him for his cheery attitude, his grit, and his perseverance.

Later, they had a fulfilling exercise in which they went around the circle and each person told their teammates what they appreciated about them. Each person had a turn on the "hot seat," and all they could say in response to this praise was "thank you." It may not seem like much, but imagine the impact if each member of your team were to tell you something they sincerely appreciated about you. You certainly would not forget what they said or how you felt in that moment. Alternatively, your ability to take the time to assure what every member of your team means to you will encourage a culture of respect and appreciation.

The result of the exercise was a team that reinforced their common purpose—that is, to accomplish goals *together*. And they recognized that struggles present opportunities for growth and are a catalyst for building trust. The evening concluded with the acknowledgment that trust is fragile and, like a garden, needs constant care, weeding, and watering. And that was the team's commitment, to be ever vigilant about maintaining the trust that happens between people—especially when they practice selflessness.

Engagement only comes when people believe in what they're doing and that the common purpose supports a higher purpose—be that a duty to a teammate, or a focus externally on making a difference in the lives of others. As a sales manager one of us worked for said, "Leadership is simple. I help you get what you want, and you will help me get what I want." What he meant was that leaders must understand individual drivers, or motivators, in order to get a group of individuals working together and reach a goal that can only be accomplished through teamwork. That doesn't happen without intention with regard to how the leader wants people to feel when they're asked to expend even more energy.

The morning after the bonfire, the team reached the summit without incident, but the real achievement was the camaraderie formed at base camp. It was the pause, the reset, the demonstration of truly selfless actions that made the difference. The CEO definitely played a pivotal role, but the success came from the sense of duty the team had for each other. The group who got the fire going wasn't made up of necessarily the most selfless people, but those who had the energy at that particular moment. A high performing team intuitively knows that leadership shows up when the unique situation aligns with specific strengths. Some people knew how to get a fire going, others knew where to look for wood, and some knew the best way to create tinder from wet wood that would catch the spark (or, in this case, the "flamethrower"!). The intentional stop—the base camp—is what made all the difference. If the team had been pushed to keep going through the night, safety might have been an issue, but morale, for certain, would have suffered.

**PRO TIP**

Make sure you are intentional and deliberate with rest so you can reenergize your team and boost engagement. Remember the "levers" of structure, process, incentives, and people, and how linked and interdependent they are. Culture must support strategy—not the other way around. Help your people find deep purpose and meaning in what they do to serve others, and the value they provide. Consider asking your team—how does your day-to-day work improve people's lives?

Now take a moment to consider your own organization and how you approach your base camp:

- What are three observable behaviors you can reinforce around the value of *selflessness* when your team is reflecting, reenergizing, and reengaging?
- What are three observable behaviors you can reinforce around the value of *courage* when your team is reflecting, reenergizing, and reengaging?
- What are three observable behaviors you can reinforce around the value of *discipline* when your team is reflecting, reenergizing, and reengaging?

## THE REST OF THE STORY

As they finished their supper, Jared and Doug sat silently in their tent. It was obvious that dinner conversation was off the table, so to speak, because the wind was so loud they would have had to scream to hear each other despite being inches apart. After getting some hot food in their stomachs, they ventured out one more time to relieve themselves before they bunked down for the night. (Peeing in sixty-mile-per-hour winds requires a few adjustments, as you might imagine!) As Jared started to nod off, Doug gave him a good-natured punch in the arm for laughing at him when he was floating and screaming. They both knew his magic carpet ride would be a story that would get told, and exaggerated, for years to come.

## CONCLUSION

Base camp isn't the finish line, just another starting point. When a leader uses intentional rest to create a pace that's doable, the team has the place and space to reenergize and reengage. It's been said that cars have brakes so you can go fast. The effective leader knows that, as we say, sometimes you have to slow down to speed up. What's your base camp equivalent? Have you created times and places to reenergize and reengage? It might be nice to go fast all the time, but it's not practical. We have to manage our energy and the energy of those around us. As we say when we reach a summit: "Okay. We're here, which is great, but see that other peak over there? What would it take for us to get there?"

To ensure that when your team hits its goals they're reenergized, and ready to reengage for that next big, hairy, audacious one, base camp is a necessity; a deliberate and well-planned rest and a chance to acknowledge appreciation for the effort and progress thus far. It's easy to lose sight of others when you're moving up a mountain, or working on big goals, but as Mother Teresa said, "Never be so busy as not to think of others."

## THE THREE PILLARS

### *Leading Self*

Everyone has a responsibility to prepare for the next day, next project, or next obstacle. You need to invest in your own mental, physical, and emotional well-being so you have the energy to assist and help others.

- Conduct an energy audit. How are you doing mentally, physically, and emotionally on a scale of 1–10? What would it take for you to improve in each area?
- Given the next project or challenge on the horizon, what can you do today to get ready?
- How are you living your values—what you stand for and support? Cite specific behaviors that others could observe.

### *Leading Others*

Communal duties are paramount. Leading others is about creating a collective sense of duty to ensure that the entire team's capabilities and capacity are realized, allowing for the achievement of aspirational goals. If a single hero emerges, it's likely that the team has failed to work as a unit.

- When your team reflects on this time together in the future, what do you want them to say about the culture?
- What can you do to further show you care for each and every teammate?
- Are there any in-groups and out-groups on your team? If so, how can you work to create one team?

### *Leading the Organization*

Base camp is ultimately a design opportunity, a chance for the leader to develop the most effective culture and environment, one in which the team works together to accomplish set goals. A supportive organization doesn't come about by chance—you need to lead the way.

- How can you create a culture where people not only can, but are expected to, reenergize?
- In which ways do you share the responsibility of leadership with others to leverage talents and maximize engagement?
- What tasks do you need to accomplish so the organization is truly prepared for and committed to the next big challenge?

CHAPTER 6

# FIRESIDE CHAT

## *Accelerating Relationships*

> "In a safe environment you should share your context and perspective and hear how others perceive it differently. This is where vulnerability and authenticity are important."
>
> —*Waldo Waldman, Hall of Fame Speaker and Veteran Participant, Wallowa Mountains, Oregon*

Reflecting on the last day in Patagonia, Devin, an information security executive, remembered that the weather was just miserable. "It was cold and windy with freezing rain and sleet coming down in sheets." He explained, "There was nothing around us, no animals, no safety network, nothing. We were truly on our own. We reached a point in the trek where we had to slow down as the path narrowed; and the guides were seeking input from us on which route to take. They could have decided for us, but they wanted us to weigh in, to take ownership for how we were doing. Nobody objected, so I didn't either, even though I had some reservations."

That evening, when the time came for everyone to gather around in a circle to reflect on the day, another participant said, "My hands are freezing. I hate when it's raining *and* cold!" You could hear the collective sigh of relief, as he stated what everyone else had been thinking, including Devin. As he pointed out, "Everyone had been afraid to bring it up, fearing they'd be perceived as invoking one of 'the three Cs' we had established as ground rules: no condemning, criticizing, or complaining. Acknowledging that shared misery, despite breaking the rules this once, actually brought the team closer together."

That simple comment, enabled by a reflective fireside chat, was a demonstration of humility and vulnerability. It created an opportunity for the team to reflect on their own self-reliance, which meant taking ownership of their mental, emotional, and physical well-being. A fellow teammate confessed that he didn't believe the team members, including himself, had been honest throughout the day about their level of discomfort. Though keeping their pain to themselves did not result in severe injury this time, it could have—frostbite is a nasty problem to deal with—and it would have jeopardized the whole team and expedition. Everyone sitting around the campfire that night took away a memorable lesson: people won't always tell you when they're struggling.

The impact of this direct feedback led participants to open up with each other in a way they hadn't earlier in the day. They listened carefully to each other's reflections on the distances they had climbed and covered, and they began to realize how far they had come as individuals, and as a team. These conversations occur at the end of the day fireside, a time and place where people are a little stinky, a little bruised (sometimes a knee, sometimes an ego), more than a little tired, and incredibly thankful. The fireside chat is not just a rundown of the day's activities, but an opportunity to reflect and bond. Early on, teammates are often nervous about having something insightful to say. Some rely on humor, sharing ghost stories and jokes. Others quickly dig into serious topics like their personal and professional lives.

We often fail to slow down enough for reflection, and we rarely take the time to hear and understand the perspectives of others. In our day-to-day life, people won't always tell us when they are struggling, when they need help, or when they have an issue they need to discuss or resolve. When people are exhausted, though, they tend to let down their guard and are often more forthcoming. As a leader, it is your responsibility to foster a culture where people can speak their truth, in the absence of exhaustion.

When team members pause to hear each other's stories on an expedition, they sometimes find radically different perspectives on the day's events, causing them to wonder if they are even on the same trek. This pause is absolutely necessary, as it allows the opportunity to understand and empathize with an individual and ultimately help the team thrive. Personal reflection may be a first step, but listening to others is critical.

As a leader, you need to be open to others' perspectives and diverse points of view. However, you won't know what those are unless you take the time to truly listen to your team members, and then pepper them with follow-up questions to eliminate your own assumptions and truly understand them. People often hide their emotions or true feelings behind humor, or a protective façade, not allowing the people they work with every single day to know who they really are, and what they really think. When we turn on our curiosity, what the illusionist Harris III calls the "wonder-switch," we create magical breakthroughs that allow us to lead better and form more effective teams.

A "fireside chat" creates the space for these "wonder-switch" moments as teams co-create a coherent narrative based upon different experiences throughout the trek. The ultimate aim is to reflect on the day to learn, build trust, and improve individual and team performance with discipline and grit. In the process, the team's relationships and one's leadership capabilities are accelerated. Being open and curious, asking great questions, and pausing to hear others' responses can help you better make sense of your experience and emotions.

This can only take place when you first take off your own mask and are honest with the person in the mirror. If you do, then your team will be honest with you in return, and with each other. Trust is built when everyone is willing to open themselves up by being more vulnerable, which requires a delicate balance of confidence and humility. In the process, a wider, more diverse range of voices will be shared, heard, and incorporated into improving individual commitment and the organization's culture. This goal is at the heart of an organization committed to learning, and it begins with leaders who create an environment where people feel safe enough to explore their effect on others.

## LAYING THE GROUNDWORK

We cover ground rules extensively prior to the expedition, and reinforce seven ground rules that are particularly important when it comes to the fireside chat. They can be used in any setting when a discussion takes place about what happened during a given day, project, or exercise. These rules ensure everyone feels respected, heard, and open to sharing, and they work equally as well at high elevations as they do in conference rooms.

- **Be Punctual.** It's a sign of respect when meetings predictably start and end on time. When you have to wait on a teammate or repeat what's already been said when someone arrives late, they have wasted the team's time. You risk not getting to everything that needs to be covered and running long, which impacts your team's other responsibilities and tasks. Coordination and collaboration happens in meetings; work happens outside of them.

- **Participate.** In a fireside chat, everyone is obligated to speak up and share their insights and perspectives. People count on their teammates to help the team become more effective and cohesive. If someone is as quiet as a church mouse, they stunt others' ability to learn through a robust discussion. If fear is holding someone back from contributing, worrying they don't have value to add, help them recognize that others might feel the same way about themselves as well. It can help people realize everyone else on the team is contributing, even though they have similar reservations.
- **Have One Conversation.** When teammates are all in on the same conversation, magic happens. Sidebar conversations, however, can ruin that magic. Not only are they rude to the person speaking, but they distract those who are trying to listen, cheating the entire team out of potential insights. When we are all in together, we learn together.
- **Risk Saying What You Think.** As mentioned in chapter three, to risk saying what you think, while also holding your views lightly, requires you to balance your authentic self and remain sensitive to the impact of your words. This can be a tough thing to do. Balancing authenticity, vulnerability, and boldness with biases and assumptions is difficult for all of us. By seeking to understand where others are coming from, everyone can feel empowered to speak their thoughts and opinions without fear. To earn the right to share your true perspective requires you to show people that you first care deeply about them as individuals. The most effective feedback in fireside chats tends to be when participants are willing to challenge their teammates directly while holding care and concern for their teammate in high regard.
- **Be Kind and Inclusive.** Kind is different than nice. Kindness is expressed through the actions you take for other people,

while nice can involve superficial words and gestures. Kind, for example, is delivering a tough message. Nice is a sympathetic and softhearted sentiment that tiptoes around what the other person really needs to hear. Inclusive means it's everyone's job to bring all the voices into the conversation. This could include piggybacking comments off of others rather than changing the conversation. It might be asking a follow-up question, or asking someone who has been quiet to weigh in with their unique perspective.

- **Keep Confidential Conversations Confidential.** In fireside chats, what's discussed is private and not to be shared outside the group without permission. Nothing kills trust in a team more than gossip. While you may want to share a particular lesson, you can do so without sharing a person's story or any sensitive comments. Share the learning, not the narrative.
- **Remain Aware.** Appreciate the beauty of the surroundings, including how light and weather change the view and your perspective, and how the external environment applies to other areas of life, including how we view others. Put simply: be present. One major advantage of the Crucibles is you have no cell phone reception, forcing you to be in the moment, a gift we seldom have in today's hyper-connected world. It truly allows you to gift someone your undivided attention. When you are present, you can listen to understand versus listen to merely respond. Even if that sometimes means you may forget what you wanted to say, that's okay! The point is to stay connected in the moment.

There may be one or two other ground rules that are important for your organization or team, depending on your goals, industry, or particular work culture. With that in mind, you can use the ones outlined here as a starting point and tailor them to what best fits your situation and circumstances. And make sure the expectations are clear for your fireside chats.

Once the ground rules are understood and agreed to, create clarity about what will be discussed. By giving the conversation structure, teammates can better gather their thoughts and prepare for both meaningful contributions and deep listening. As the structure becomes routine, you will find a flywheel emerges. The conversations can get to the heart of the learning moments and deepen relationships even faster. There are two main elements or parts of the fireside chat: the review of the day and a leadership discussion.

## REVIEW OF THE DAY

Reviewing the day can also be referred to as an After Action Review (AAR), hotwash, debrief, briefback, feedback loop, post-mortem, or even a retrospective analysis. Regardless of what you call it at your organization, the process can be used after the completion of a project, to close out a financial quarter, an update meeting, or any other milestone, small or large. Reflection in any form provides the opportunity to dig down into not just what happened, and its outcome, but how it affected each member of the team individually and collectively.

During a Crucible, the nightly review of the day is facilitated by the person who was the leader for the day. The best leader-facilitators ask probing and insightful questions, and then hold back to let the group answer. Less effective leaders try to ask and answer all the questions themselves—not surprisingly, this overbearing style tends to stifle insights and perspectives from the rest of the team. The best leaders also break down the conversation into small segments, ensuring all aspects of the trek are covered and details, even those that initially seem unimportant, aren't skimmed over. A segment might include the time in the morning when everyone is packing for the day, the beginning of the trek, the lunch break, the time setting up for the night, or any other easily recognizable portion of the trek.

At the start of the review, it's important to discuss what *actually* took place. This is the time for people to be brutally honest and open. There is no judgment here, just facts about what was observed and how people felt. Unpacking what, how, and why things happened allows us to uncover what we can do to be more effective in future circumstances. You can imagine Devin's team talking about waking up to freezing rain and sleet and thinking through the way they packed up camp, plotted their route, and moved along their path. As the path narrowed and the guides asked for their input on which route to take, the team abdicated ownership by merely following the guides.

Perhaps teammates recognized many of them were "over it" and assumed the guides would take them back the fastest way possible, or they lacked confidence in their ability to read the maps. Perhaps they were concerned they might actually make the trek harder on the team. In the debrief, they would likely recognize that expressing these thoughts in the moment would have actually helped the team collectively process a decision point. By sharing openly in the fireside chat, they better understand themselves and each other when they tackle the next day.

Back at the office, knowing a teammate may tend to become merely compliant when they run out of energy could help you recognize when you need to reschedule a meeting that requires everyone on the team to be "all in." Or individually, if you recognize this trait in yourself, you'll know you have to dig deep to find the energy required for such a meeting. Furthermore, AARs allow you to be better prepared to have authentic conversations about your team's understanding of how the strategy was selected and when it's best for them to weigh in and add their perspectives. By owning their responsibility to discuss, debate, and ultimately commit to decisions, they can propel the project, team, and even organization forward.

During the review of the day, after discussing what happened, the team is instructed to look at what went well. Each response is followed by asking, "What else?" As the leader, you want to emphasize the positive attributes of the experience because, in short order, you'll be discussing what could have been better. What went right with Devin's team? They happily shared how they saw each and every member of the team dig deep. Each of them was exhausted, and looking around, they saw that same feeling in their teammates' faces and movements. So they all realized they had to embrace their own self-reliance, as they knew no one had much left in their tank to pick up anyone else's slack. In the process, recognizing they were each dependable and reliable made the entire team feel secure. Unfortunately, many high performing teams gloss over what went well because they are eager to point out what didn't. But by dwelling on what went right, you provide the encouragement they'll need next time they run out of energy.

When discussing what didn't work out quite right, the team, and the leader, must reflect on their own shortcomings. In doing so, they identify what they are then accountable to improve upon, and they openly discuss this with each other. Note that individual negative feedback should only be what was personally observed, not something shared with one team member by another participant. Secondhand observations only lead to misrepresentations, misunderstanding, and mistrust.

If a team falls into the pattern of the three Cs—condemning, criticizing, or complaining—learning and innovation are hampered, as the team may overemphasize what went wrong and perhaps lose the lessons from what went well. This situation can also create an environment of fear. When it comes to the three Cs, condemning is the apex of this trifecta. When you condemn a teammate, you write them off, giving them no pathway to build a meaningful relationship with you. When you criticize, it's the opposite of providing constructive feedback. It makes people defensive. Complaining is the least threatening of the three Cs, but it can have a profound impact on your ability to lead yourself. When we complain, we are focused on the negative, a scarcity versus abundance mindset. Positive mindsets are needed to see the best in others and the potential solutions for the myriad of problems we face every day.

The final step of the review is to discuss what the team will do differently going forward. Adaptability requires the willingness to adjust, turning problems into opportunities. This is the time when expectations are realigned and commitment made on what the team agreed to do better and differently. In effect, this step is about change management, which is creating strong alliances to work together with purpose and resolve.

## LEADERSHIP DISCUSSION

The review of the day helps the team tactically break down the details of what happened, what went well, and where they have opportunity for growth, personally and collectively. If the discussion ended there, it would be a successful learning moment and bonding experience as people provide meaningful feedback to each other. But there is more to gain from the time spent in a fireside chat. After the review of the day, the floor is opened to talk about what team members have on their mind in relation to their experience that day and leadership in general.

These leadership discussions are a core part of the fireside chat, but they can also become unfocused grumble sessions. Participants are therefore asked to pay attention to both the content and the dynamic of the conversation as it progresses. When expertly facilitated, there are typically six directions the discussion can go that can ultimately lead to a high level of engagement and learning.

- **Dispute.** It's all right to dispute or challenge assumptions, provided it's done with dignity and respect. During these discussions, some pretty heated conversations can take place, especially when people are unaware of their biases. On one Crucible, the tension was palpable when one person generalized his observations regarding certain people he had worked with. His biases were quickly, and vocally, disputed by other team members' opinions, feelings, and presentation of facts. He came away with an awareness and appreciation for checking his assumptions, "reading the room," and seeking to ask questions to understand where other people stood on their values and beliefs. In these conversations, make sure ground rules are followed regarding how people treat each other with dignity and respect. Sometimes the leader has to have the courage to call out biases or poor judgment. Most of the time, this is best done in private, but there are times when you need to send a clear signal to the group that what was just said is not okay. This is not to chastise the speaker, but to help them understand how their delivered words were felt by the group, regardless of "best intentions."

- **Disagree.** To disagree is okay, but to be disagreeable is not. Don't allow people to throw a disagreement out without the *why*. Instead, get them to dig deep, and explain to the group why they disagree. They need to first help others understand where they're coming from, sharing their observations, focus, interpretations, and assumptions, and how those inform their conclusion and beliefs. They are also asked to do the same thing in reverse; that is, to understand where other people are coming from by asking the person they disagree with about their observations, focus, interpretations, and assumptions. This part of the discussion helps people develop empathy, which is required to disagree respectfully.
- **Debate.** As French moralist Joseph Joubert observed, "It is better to debate a question without settling it than to settle a question without debating it. For good ideas and true innovation, you need human interaction, conflict, argument, debate."

During one leadership discussion, the topic of ego came up. Teammates quickly took sides. In one camp were those who felt a little ego helped you be audacious. The other side felt ego gets in the way of humility. Through the discussion, the group settled on the fact that for ego to serve as a desirable trait, it has to be accompanied by self-awareness, along with just the right balance of confidence and humility. In business, debating issues can bring alternative perspectives and facts to light. Debate is also a sure sign that the leader has created a safe environment. No debate? There's probably complacency or fear, neither of which can be present in an indomitable team.

- **Consensus.** Sometimes an issue will be raised during these discussions that requires a decision, one on which it is perhaps best to reach consensus. The aim is for consensus to follow debate, especially with regard to tough decisions. Reaching consensus can be tricky because you don't want groupthink, but you also don't want a stalemate either. It's important to state the goal of consensus up front and the process by which it's reached. For example, with a Crucible, when a tough decision needs to be made—like whether to climb to summit A, summit B, or don't summit at all—everyone's opinion is appreciated. The leader summarizes those opinions, and says, "It sounds like the consensus is summit A, so here's what we're going to do . . ." This part of the discussion almost always leads to better commitment, especially when the going gets tough along the way.
- **Commit.** When the leader states the direction after consensus, the group is asked to unite behind the decision. There was healthy debate, and everyone had a voice, but now's the time to get behind the team—even if you stated reasons for why you disagreed. Engagement and true commitment lead to exceeding

expectations and achieving high performance standards. Performance is a combination of results and behaviors aligned with expectations usually expressed by the core values of the group.

- **Collaborate.** Once the team makes a commitment to the path forward, they need to collaborate through all aspects of the endeavor—or what most call execution. This means excellent communication and healthy conflict, as described earlier in this section. Effective teams still have dynamic relationships—there is no stasis when it comes to working with people. You're either making deposits with relationships, or you're making withdrawals. The more deposits, the more trust. The more trust, the more camaraderie. And there is nothing more fulfilling and rewarding than working toward a common goal with a commitment to collaboration resulting in great camaraderie.

Besides a general discussion on leadership in which insights are gained, another outcome from robust debate and discussion is team trust. A guest from *The Leadership Podcast*, author, executive, and speaker Louis Efron, said, "If you're talking about trust, it probably doesn't exist."[1] Once a team has trust, they can tackle almost any topic together; without it, they can tackle almost nothing.

## RECOGNIZING RESPONSIBILITY

A young army lieutenant was once asked, rather sarcastically, "So now that you've led a platoon, and know everything there is to know about leadership, what have you learned?" The young officer paused, and said, "You have to really care about your people. If you care, you will listen. If you listen, you will know their hopes and desires and dreams. You will actually know what motivates them. Then, and only then, can you hope to inspire and guide them to be the best version of themselves." A pretty good answer, and a justification for being truly curious about others' values, assumptions, beliefs, and expectations.

That curiosity to really listen, and possibly change course, requires vulnerability. And vulnerability begets vulnerability—if someone lets down their shield, others will do the same. As a Crucible participant once expressed their sense of duty to others, "I was always nervous that I wouldn't have something insightful to say, but I fought to listen carefully and ensure my comments were additive, not just mirroring someone else." Another participant commented: "It was interesting to learn how on the same page you are with everyone else, because other people expressed their struggles, which created the opportunity to really bond." Leadership can be lonely if you let it. You may be going through something all by yourself, but there are always other people who can relate, empathize, and encourage. That will only happen if you're willing to put yourself in situations where you're comfortable opening up and, even if it's scary for you, asking for help.

During the fireside chat, participants are encouraged to admit and take ownership of their mistakes. But there is a common rationalization of behavior that confuses blame with responsibility. It holds that people are only responsible for dealing with problems they created. Bad things might not be your fault, but now that you're involved (especially as a leader), the situation or crisis is definitely your responsibility. On a Crucible, it could mean someone lost a glove or a hat, and the notion being that person should "suck it up" versus someone taking the time to figure out if someone else brought extras or fashion gloves from a pair of thick socks. This approach bears out in that people begin to realize they are responsible for teammates: duty-bound to one another—sometimes even at a personal cost. Once the expectations are set with how important it is to be curious and vulnerable, the job of the leader is to facilitate the fireside chat. Like most aspects of leading others, it's all about articulating the expectations, covering the ground rules, and setting the tone.

## THE REST OF THE STORY

The last fireside chat in Patagonia was actually done during the afternoon, because there was no wood to gather for a fire, and the nights were bitter cold! During that particular chat, the team again circled around and remarked how positive everyone had been during the trek. Not one person showed up as "Negative Ned," and brought down the team. People took responsibility for their own well-being, because each person understood that it was part of their duty to ensure the team performed at a high level. The lead guide remarked that they had all experienced "what Patagonia was all about—a beautiful, but harsh and unforgiving environment." Collectively, the team recognized that everyone was "sucking at some point," but knew that by openly sharing their quiet suffering, they would have brought down the morale of the team. Yet, the group saw what makes an indomitable team, and that they are all capable of doing much more than they thought they could—especially when they worked together, serving others before serving themselves.

### PRO TIP

President Truman famously had a placard on his desk that read, "The buck stops here." As a leader, you are ultimately responsible for everything the team does or fails to do; the buck stops with you. When leaders fully recognize and embrace that awesome responsibility, they can eliminate the need to "find blame," and instead get after the real work of solving problems. Taking personal ownership, even if the problem originated elsewhere, also sets an example to the organization that everyone is fallible and can reflect, learn, and adapt.

Now take a moment to consider your own organization and how you approach your fireside chats:

- Is two-way communication centered on curiosity?
- Does respect and trust exist at all levels?
- Are mistakes viewed as opportunities for learning, growth, innovation, and development?

## CONCLUSION

The fireside chat helps build the trust that's so foundational to whether the organization norms, storms, and ultimately performs. If you effectively create a trusting environment in your fireside chats to allow for openness, vulnerability, and curiosity, you can tackle the hard issues that are sure to arise. Trust allows teams to dispute, disagree, and debate, then commit to the team's decision as a collaborative and unified front, even if it's not the call an individual teammate would have made on their own. The better the team is able to tackle tough issues (because of strong and duty-bound relationships), the faster the team can accelerate and efficiently execute the mission.

Incorporating the "fireside chat" as a disciplined approach to reviewing both the outcomes and the relationships of the team is a surefire way to accelerate trust and forge an indomitable team. As the leader, it's your responsibility to spell out the expectation that leading self means displaying curiosity and being vulnerable. You must also effectively set ground rules. A fireside chat is an opportunity to elicit a diverse range of perspectives that are shared and heard. They can then be incorporated into improving trust, gaining commitment, and enhancing the organization's culture through unassailable bonds of social capital. Those are the bonds that allow you to effectively achieve a common purpose.

## THE THREE PILLARS

### *Leading Self*

The fireside chat can be a powerful tool to help you understand what happened, the positive or negative role you played in the outcome, and the impact on others. It is also a time for you to reflect on your own experience and emotions around the journey.

- Are the stories people tell about the experience aligning with yours? How are they similar, or different?
- Are you proud of how you showed up in the experience? What would you change moving forward?
- Have others misread your intentions? If so, why do you think that happened?

### *Leading Others*

Leaders don't always get it right when setting up a conversation for true learning and connection. Establishing a safe environment for people to bring all they have to offer is a critical part of facilitating fireside chats.

- Given the members of your team, what are some clear ground rules you can establish for the behaviors and norms during fireside chats?
- How can you encourage everyone to speak up and contribute to the growth of the team?
- Are there any team dynamics or conflicts that must be addressed before your team can create a collaborative space where it's safe to be vulnerable?

### *Leading the Organization*

Unfortunately, fear is one of the most common emotions people experience at work. When we're afraid, we don't see the big picture, and our creative capacity diminishes. It's important that a trusting environment exists where people can be vulnerable, where they can speak up, know they matter, and feel they belong.

- Do teammates regularly place others' needs or interests over their own?
- How do teammates define "being a team player" in their job?
- When people take responsibility for a bad decision, mistake, or failure, how does that land with others on the team?

CHAPTER 7

# WHO'S WHO?

## *Cultivating the Group Dynamic*

"Being in an environment where you have nothing to prove, protect, or promote helped us meet the challenges starting on day one. When you let go of preconceived notions about yourself, it was a really interesting environment to be in. Your title, level, fitness, experience, etc., didn't matter. We all had to accomplish the tasks together."

—*Julie Keller, Executive Participant, Moab, Utah*

About nine thousand feet above sea level, on the side of Aneroid Mountain in the Wallowa Mountains of eastern Oregon, two teams were trying to reach the summit in two very different ways. One team took a direct path that, it seemed, would get them to the summit much more quickly than the other, but the route involved steep cliffs with greater exposure—places where a slip could result in a fall and serious injury. The other team decided to take a longer route with little to no exposure, but it would certainly mean more distance and more time.

It wasn't until they were midway through their route that the *cautious* team could see the *riskier* team up ahead. They conceded the riskier team would reach the peak an hour earlier, but the leader of the team reminded them they were still going to make it to the top; and they'd have the added benefit of actually enjoying the trip along the way. What the cautious team didn't know was that the riskier team had stopped. They were making no forward progress at all. The exposure had put the fear of God into a few team members and they were completely stalled, loudly "negotiating" with each other—or, in other words, arguing. They couldn't agree on whether to descend and take another route, or push through while exposing themselves to a series of steep ledges.

The riskier team's leader charged ahead, with little effective collaboration or communication with the team on the planned route, and no discussion of the risks involved. After some time, a number of team members spoke up, loudly expressing complaints and unmitigated, immobilizing fears. Everyone's mood and morale took a hit. Meanwhile, the cautious team's members were smiling, laughing, and taking frequent breaks. Their leader was entirely open with them, and frequently sought their input on the route of travel, pace, and overall tone of the team's spirit.

The combination of personalities during such a difficult pursuit draws out different strengths and weaknesses of those involved, especially when everyone is feeling stressed. A person from the cautious team may have played a different role on the riskier team, and vice versa. It's the same at work—whether it's a project, a sales campaign, or the development of a new product. Unique roles allow people's natural tendencies to emerge to the benefit, or detriment, of the team. Cultivating the group dynamic means figuring out who's who, and that's much easier (and happens faster) when presented with difficulties.

By paying attention to the group dynamic, you can better encourage others to use their strengths and natural tendencies to both find where within the group they can best contribute and how they can grow from these experiences. This approach allows team members to push themselves outside their comfort zone, developing new skills and talents in the process, and exhibiting a sense of duty to put the team first, even if they are uncomfortable. The mindset here must be that, "Part of my job is making everyone else's job easier—not harder." You need to nurture self-awareness in yourself, leading to the same feeling of psychological safety that the team must develop. This feeling of safety comes first from your own self-awareness, and then through developing trust in the people you must come to rely on.

## GROUP DYNAMICS

We've all been there. You're the new person. You're nervous because you want to make a good first impression. So many unknowns: "Will I like these people? Will they like me?" "Did I make the right decision to leave my old job?" Ultimately, when we're new to a team we ask ourselves, "Will these new people care about me as a person? Will my job matter?" These insecurities are common, human, and predictable.

Knowing that people join a team with such insecurities, it's up to you as the leader to keep confidence and humility balanced with individuals and the team. We all need a certain amount of swagger and sense of adventure at times to help us believe in ourselves, but we also need humility to keep our ego in check. Some of us are more confident than humble, and others are more humble than confident. Humans are a complex bunch, but by recognizing some of the common behaviors you can expect from your team's dynamic, you will be better equipped to help your people succeed at the tasks at hand.

### *Expected Behaviors*

As participants trek through the wilderness, with varying degrees of physical preparedness and discomfort, they take on different roles. Those up front scout, point out obstacles, highlight safety concerns, and provide direction and rerouting as needed. The people in the middle trudge along, focused on keeping the pace so as not to create gaps between team members. They are generally the most talkative people in the group, their conversations usually migrating from humorous to personal to professional. It's interesting that the personal conversations precede the professional ones, as if people have things to get off their chest before they can think about how they deal with some of the professional challenges they're facing. They either laugh and joke loudly, or speak in hushed tones, as they share and bare some of their most private thoughts. Participants in the back also play an integral role, assisting the stragglers and those struggling, whether physically, emotionally, or both. These people generally tend to be the caregivers, those who are mentally and physically strong, and who want a view from the back so they can continually assess individuals and the overall group dynamic.

These roles aren't designated by the leader. Based on the individuals, people gravitate toward their comfort zones without even thinking about it, finding where they feel they can add the most value, and be valued. Unless asked, few people on the Crucibles change their role as the trek proceeds. It's kind of like where people sit in a classroom or meeting on day one—they usually take the same seats day after day from then on. (Probably the same at your dinner table, too!) A good facilitator will push people out of their comfort zones and move them around, which benefits the group and breaks down little silos that could otherwise turn into big silos.

Generally, people up front are the overachievers; those in the middle are the extroverts; and the people in the back are the introverts. An excellent leader pays attention to the roles their team members migrate to based on their skills, experiences, and the situation at hand. This awareness helps them deploy the teammates in the future in a more deliberate fashion, based on specific objectives and timelines.

There are multiple concerns to keep in mind when creating an environment where the *who's who* on your team is sorted out. If you simply ask your team members what they bring to the team, they'll usually talk about their functional expertise. But ask them what sort of unique role, ideas, or perspectives they can provide, and the strength and diversity of the team will start to emerge. The team will begin evolving before they start performing at a high level, but it's not always a smooth process.

Research from psychologist and author Ron Friedman shows the lubricant for friction when there is more traction than drag can be increased through a number of disciplined practices. As Friedman explains, "creating a high-performing workplace takes more than simply hiring the right people and arming them with the right tools to do their work. It requires creating opportunities for genuine, authentic relationships to develop."[1] It is as simple and as complex as what happens between people—the actual human relationship and social capital that has the potential to yield extraordinary results.

Oftentimes, people generally describe themselves as introverts or extroverts. But that label doesn't really matter when it comes to the team dynamic. The only real difference between introverts and extroverts is where they get their energy. Introverts recharge with downtime, often spent alone. Extroverts recharge by being social, spending time with others. In either case, this trait has nothing to do with who will be boisterous and who might be passive. On Crucibles, the quieter participants tend to be astute listeners and have poignant insights when it comes to seeing and appreciating others' strengths.

Another trait often self-identified early on is that of being an overachiever. On one hand, Crucible participants are all accomplished individuals. On the other hand, they can be perfectionists, and they sometimes struggle with setting priorities and realizing that not everything has to be *just right*. Overachievers are also the ones who may get "summit fever"—they can lose sight of safety concerns and others' well-being because they're so focused on achieving the objective.

By digging deeper, however, you can help people identify their unique traits that will benefit the whole team. Those who demonstrate true self-awareness, often with your input, will recognize which of the following roles they will best serve in, or adapt to, while on this particular team:

- **Energizers** operate with a sense of urgency and, as pacesetters, keep the team on schedule. They recognize when to take a break and when to step on the gas.
- **Coordinators** focus on ensuring the team cooperates, collaborates, and reaches consensus. They're the ones who are most cognizant of tone and how the team is feeling at any given moment.
- **Implementers** focus on execution and putting ideas into action. They ensure the direction is followed. They're the pragmatic ones, who will make sure things get done according to the standard based on what the team values.
- **Innovators** suggest new ideas and approaches that make the team more effective, efficient, and productive.
- **Analyzers** are objective and analytical, ensuring the team focuses as much on the quantitative as the qualitative. They help the team see the metrics of progress, or lack thereof.

- **Challengers** seek continuous improvement for the team by questioning decisions and actions. They might be prickly, but they're the outlier the team needs to avoid groupthink.

These roles can serve to create balance for the team. The energizer sets the pace, and the coordinator provides feedback on whether the pace is too fast or too slow. The implementer sets the direction, and the innovator suggests other alternatives. The analyzer provides the metrics based on prior decisions to what's working—and what's not working—and fuel for the challenger. Some roles slow the team down with a thoughtful and deliberate approach. Others are the drivers who keep the team moving forward with decisiveness. Together, they lead to collaboration, consensus, and compromise, all rolled into one dynamic entity—the team. And the leader is responsible for keeping the balance, which means no one role runs roughshod over the others. They're all equally important to maintain a degree of symbiosis.

Whether you are deciding which route to take up the side of a mountain, or which strategic path to follow for the upcoming fiscal year, having the innovator, analyzer, and coordinator collaborate on options can illuminate the best path. The implementer, energizer, and challenger then have clear roles to help the team successfully move forward and execute. To achieve that balance and success, establishing ground rules (the importance of which was discussed in chapter six) is necessary to completing tasks and achieving goals, while treating one another with dignity and respect.

Just as you need to be able to identify the general roles in which your team members best fit, you need to take the time to do some honest soul searching and consider which role you most align with as well. In some cases, your team may play to your strengths, and in others, you may have to make significant adjustments to ensure you create a successful team. One of the biggest adjustments leaders often need to make is to be more deferential. Empower your people, let them shine, give them that what and why, and let them go to town on the how.

Being deferential is especially important when communicating amid healthy conflict and decision-making. By yielding respectfully to others' thoughts, feelings, opinions, and suggestions, you will be able to receive their valuable input, instead of being so assertive you bulldoze people into submission. Being deferential, however, also slows processes down, which can test the patience of leaders operating with a high sense of urgency. Still, it helps to get buy-in from your team, securing real engagement in the long run, and requiring less supervision and follow-up. Further, being deferential builds a strong foundation for team morale and engagement.

### *Team Development*

When the challenger, implementer, energizer, coordinator, innovator, and analyzer roles come together, the team goes through five stages, as outlined by psychologist Bruce Tuckman.[2] Those stages play out as follows during the Crucibles:

- **Forming.** Forming is when participants figure out who's who, sizing up strengths, and proactively and dynamically selecting roles. The team is looking for safety and approval in this stage as they also attempt to define tasks and how decisions are to be made. It is in this stage where you will find people on their best behavior, being overly polite and not yet sharing their true ideas and opinions.
- **Storming.** The honeymoon phase of the forming stage disappears here as people begin to vie for power and influence among the team. If you're not struggling with a certain amount of conflict, there is one of two problems. The first is malaise or complacency, meaning people on the team just don't care about goals or their responsibility toward achieving them. The second

is that team members are afraid, and fear is a contagion for dysfunction. Meanwhile, friendliness can mask groupthink at this stage, so be on guard against its potential negative effects.

- **Norming.** Norming means the team is open to learning, which also means mistakes are expected and tolerated because they represent growth if dealt with constructively. When teams take the conflict from the storming stage and begin to focus their energy on finding solutions and employing effective conflict resolution, as seen through shared influence and problem-solving, they are constructively dealing with mistakes and challenges. It is here that a rhythm begins to flow.
- **Performing.** The stage is now set for an indomitable team, allowing for high performance through competence, autonomy, and a deep commitment to one another. At this point, teammates recognize when to leverage their own strengths and when to allow others to take the lead to create real value, both internally and externally. The grit and disciplined duty displayed in the earlier stages serves as a catapult for teams to hit their full stride.
- **Adjourning.** All teams come to an end either because the Crucible ends, the project is completed, or teammates leave. Indomitable teams don't let this occur without taking the time to slow down, capture lessons learned, and celebrate success. This stage is essential for creating a culture where people continue an upward trajectory of growth and feel valued in the process, because when one team ends, others are formed for subsequent goals and challenges.

In all of these stages, humor can help level the group. On expeditions, one of the ways people first test the environment is through humor. It happens fast. Someone will tell a joke as a trial balloon to see if the team laughs. Over time, the group not only develops a "group" dynamic, they also develop a "humor" dynamic. This loosens everyone up and helps them to bond more quickly. From there, they start to risk saying what they think about all sorts of matters. And people don't usually joke with people they don't like or trust.

The goal for any team is to foster the exchange of new ideas with regard to the day's challenges, and that's why the group dynamic is so critical. If you don't safely move through the storming stage, where you risk saying what you think, then you will not progress any further, and you will never become a high performing team. Humor, when properly applied, can lighten up even the tensest of situations, allowing everyone to release stress through laughter and help them efficiently and effectively move through the stages as a team.

They might tease and be sarcastic with each other, but they have earned the right through mutual trust and respect to do so; and people outside the team do not have that same right. The highest performing teams can often have a shared language that others don't understand. Sometimes the jokes, pokes, and prods can serve as the best form of feedback and can lead to behavior change by creating a little peer pressure. As one Crucible participant said, "There were a lot of cheerleaders, and everyone was encouraging, but sometimes there was too much Pollyanna. Humor is what brought people back into line."

On the Crucible, people come together as strangers, but with the knowledge that the team is temporary, they are often open to being vulnerable and sharing more than just their success and achievements. There is never group politics or drama; just a completely safe environment where people can speak their mind, share mistakes and failures, and take chances.

## ACCELERATING TEAM TRUST

A differentiator of an indomitable team is whether or not the leader can accelerate the team's development. That starts with providing clarity to a common purpose. Though this might sound simple, it is actually pretty challenging. The hard part is accelerating *trust*—getting people to do what they say they will while placing the needs of the team above those of their own. An expedition is a place where it's a little easier to accelerate trust. Imagine being roped up to the side of a cliff with someone you just met, and they're responsible for belaying you and keeping you from falling as you climb eighty feet off the ground. Climbing and belaying your partner is the first challenge for many Crucible participants, and if someone has a fear of heights (and many do), it's pretty hard to conceal. The question is, can they trust their teammates enough to confidently climb the side of a cliff, knowing their teammates literally have their life in their hands?

Tom was the oldest teammate on his Crucible, and the biggest. Imagine a heavyweight boxer. He was nervous about the height of the wall he had to climb and concerned about whether or not his partner, Aaron, who was much smaller than him, was capable of preventing a fall should it be needed. He gripped the wall for dear life the whole way up without ever taking in the beauty around him as he tried to overcome his near-paralyzing fear. His hands and knees were bloodied by the time his grip slipped, and Aaron caught him before he even fell more than a few inches. Any doubt that Tom had about Aaron's ability to have his back was erased, and thirty minutes was all it took to build indomitable trust.

At the office, it's critical you approach the creation of trust with intentionality. You have to ask, "What can I do to create a collective sense of duty to one another?" To accomplish this goal, you must help develop the following basic attributes among the team:

- **Selflessness.** By paying attention to the group dynamic, you can reinforce behaviors that encourage selflessness. This may be especially relevant in the storming stage when teammates are in a state of tension. Accentuate the work of your coordinators who are likely willing to sacrifice ego to collaborate or support a teammate.

- **Predictability.** Show your appreciation for people who are predictable, not erratic. Your implementers may stand out early in the forming stage as they pragmatically put ideas into action and follow through. Praise this strength of intentionality, and you'll be more deliberate about the culture you want to establish.
- **Reliability.** Get comfortable relying on team members. If they say, "Leave it with me," leave it with them. You want to show you trust the task will get done with no follow-up required. Teammates crave autonomy, and micromanagement will kill motivation. So, when innovators are charged with planning, the leader must let go and allow them to set direction, even if it is not the same path the leader would have selected. The trust demonstrated in these moments lays the foundation in the norming stage for how people work together, take initiative, and leverage each other.
- **Responsiveness.** Support team members in being prompt and approaching customer and internal issues with an appropriate sense of urgency. You are likely to find that energizers are particularly skilled in this domain, and when you help them in ways that allow them to leverage their strengths, they will know when to push the team and when to call for a break. In doing so, they amplify the team dynamics.
- **Curiosity.** Curious team members are those who want to know how their role fits into the bigger picture. They ask a lot of questions because they want to understand, prevent miscommunication, learn, and continuously improve their knowledge, along with the application of that knowledge in the form of valuable skills. This is a great description of the challengers on your team. Remember that, while at times their approach could use some tweaking, their unique attributes will serve the team's diversity of

thought. Teams who reach the performing stage have leaders who ensure that the challengers don't become the outliers and outcasts.

- **Audacity.** Audacious team members approach issues, challenges, and problems with the mindset of "If not me, who?" They take appropriate risks and challenge themselves to go above and beyond. Oftentimes when individuals don't act, it is because they lack clarity about how they fit or what they can do. Analyzers can bring strength to a team in their domain as they use their unique skills to measure risk and opportunity. These teammates provide a keen insight into capturing lessons learned and preparing for the future challenges in the adjourning stage.

When you catch people exhibiting these attributes, provide positive reinforcement. Study patterns of behavior that can be celebrated, and make note of behaviors in need of intervention. An intervention could be as simple as a suggestion via coaching, or a change to how the team is structured. By operating with a series of processes, you can keep your expectations front and center, and allow the team to develop many of these attributes on their own, simply from the problems they face and the actions they take. It's all about helping team members work together and gel more quickly as a group, while also individually learning and honing new skills to create an intentional culture of trust. But the team dynamic does not start and end with the foundational attributes above; others also require a deeper look. Let's consider each one in turn.

## *The Will to Risk*

In this chapter's opening story, a nod was given to the cautious team's approach to summiting Aneroid Mountain, but the risky team's approach had its own merits as well. Not only did they reach the summit, they also determined who on the team could really handle ambiguity, uncertainty, and stress. Handling stress with aplomb is something every team requires, which means a certain amount of stress is worth considering as an intentional design element for the group dynamic (the type of good stress discussed in chapter four).

Indomitable teams are hard to subdue or defeat—and their leaders are wired the same way. Priority one for leaders is to create an environment where there is an absence of fear, ensuring people can focus, learn, and innovate without worrying about doing or saying the "wrong" thing. That environment is one in which people will know it's okay to take risks, be adventurous, and even be bold. Bold to fail. To make mistakes. To say, "I don't know," or "I don't understand." To make decisions without perfect information. As tennis great and women's rights activist Billie Jean King said, "Be bold. If you're going to make an error, make a doozy, and don't be afraid to hit the ball."[3]

When individuals are willing to take risks, then collectively, the team will assume risks that provide the greatest return on time, energy, and dollars. Teams that have a bias to action will use untested methods, knowing full well they may not succeed at first. But a bias to action also allows them to pilot novel ideas, test their assumptions, and approach business decisions more like a scientist than a banker. They'll experiment over and over again to see what works, as compared to strictly analyzing the risk for one big, bold move.

These teams create options, discuss pros and cons, select and pivot, then position and deliver. In the process, they discover which assumptions hit and which ones missed. Then they debrief, adjust, and try again—all in rapid fashion. Abject failure only takes place if no lesson was learned. When a team is willing and courageous enough to push themselves, they can enhance individual capabilities and develop more team capacity. Nothing worth achieving is easy, and it always requires an adventurous degree of discomfort, sacrifice, and disciplined duty.

### *Authenticity*

Google's Project Aristotle was an internal research initiative designed to figure out what makes for an effective team. The multi-year study analyzed data from an array of Google teams to identify common characteristics of high performing teams, such as psychological safety, dependability, structure and clarity, and the meaning and impact of their work. The findings demonstrated the importance of creating an inclusive and collaborative team environment in which people feel safe to share ideas and work together toward common goals.

At the core, their findings boiled down to two simple traits: a safe environment where each person's voice gets equal time, and a place where people display empathy toward one another. Simply put, it's about being kind. And kindness leads to authenticity, as it allows each and every one of us to feel safe in being ourselves. Instead of needing to contort ourselves into something we are not, authentic teams help people focus on what matters: remaining engaged, committed, accountable, resourceful, resilient, humble, and disciplined. After all, if we are not being our authentic selves, what effect will that have on others?

It's not enough for one individual on the team to be authentic. Everyone has to be open and honest with themselves and the team. This requires seeing selflessness as a sense of duty to the other members: a moral obligation, responsibility, and requirement to perform and complete a task. That's the definition of duty, and effective teammates make choices based on what they *should* do versus what they *want* to do. Meanwhile, selfless leaders feel duty-bound to serve the greater good, and authenticity is the foundation of this duty.

### *Difficulties*

When we are attuned with our teammates and aware of our own abilities, we can empathetically lean into difficulties despite discomfort. When someone is engaged, committed, accountable, resourceful, resilient, humble, and disciplined, we often hear them say, "Let me carry that." During our time in the Army, we had to lug large backpacks on long marches, while also taking turns carrying additional necessary, heavy objects, whether a radio, a machine gun, or extra water. When someone said, "Let me carry that," it could be a question, or a directive, and it could have a myriad of meanings:

- *I want it now because I can see you're really struggling.*
- *You look OK now, but save your energy—don't be too proud.*
- *It's my turn; I haven't been doing my fair share.*

These messages meant the teammates were attending to the needs of others while also recognizing their ability to add value to the team. Every leader can use more of this sentiment on their team. However, "let me carry that" could also mean:

- *I am trying to be a good team player, but I really hope you keep it longer.*
- *Actually, I want to see you push yourself a bit further.*
- *My turn to be the hero.*

In such a case, teammates are being inauthentic, disempowering, or prideful. Only when the statement is coming from an authentic place of empathy and generosity does it truly have a positive impact on the team.

The other phrase that speaks volumes about a team that can deal with difficulties is, "Can you take this?" It's not only helpful to take the load when you have the energy to do so, but a selfless team with a true sense of commitment to each other knows it's expected to ask each other for help in service to the team's mission accomplishment. In fact, asking for help during difficulties is an imperative, even for the self-reliant leader. Suffering and struggling in silence will only hurt the team in the long run, so it's important to swallow your pride and ask for help. Think about how good it makes you feel when someone you respect asks for your help, filling you with a sense of usefulness and relevance.

### *Positivity vs. Negativity*

Even though there is great power in positivity when the team is wet, cold, tired, and hungry, one negative person can hurt a team more than ten positive people can help it. For that reason, positivity is even more important when adverse conditions exist on top of another obstacle, like difficult and dangerous terrain, or an individual with injury or illness. Positivity is negativity prevention. The same holds true for business. That's why negative people must be weeded out, because they're an unnecessary drain to a team. No excuse, no delay: bad apples have to go; otherwise they will become a contagion for low morale to spread. Positivity is a difficult trait to develop, but it can spread and multiply in the right environment. It just takes intentionality, especially during difficult times of stress, duress, and challenge.

People with desire are positive and driven. A collection of people who possess positivity and drive are the prerequisite for creating a team with heroic aspirations beyond power and money—a collection of souls who want to make a difference in the lives of others. But that drive has to be focused. A great team is driven—collectively and selflessly—to achieve heroic aspirations based on a common purpose facilitated by the leader. It's the drive to be extraordinary, not merely excellent; and it takes dynamic leadership focused on clearing obstacles and providing the right resources—including the right people.

## PRO TIP

To ensure clarity of the above axioms and approaches, the acronym TREE can help establish expectations:

**T**—for Team. The team comes first. Selflessness is valued over self-interest. It's a collaborative environment where trust requires compelling and unguarded debate without politics and drama.

**R**—for Results. You have to perform and hit your numbers. When you put numbers on the board, you earn influence and the ability to ask for what you want. With clarity, everyone understands the common purpose, how success is measured, and what's needed to collectively achieve the goals.

**E**—for Empathy. You need to have empathy for every position and your teammates' roles. Seek first to understand. The team must always know, "What do we need to communicate, to whom, by whom, by when?"

**E**—for make everyone's job Easier, not harder. The focus should be on your teammate, boss, customer, constituent, or partner. Internal drama not needed.

▲▲▲

Now take a moment to consider your own team and how you sort out their roles:

- How will you know the right people are in the right positions?
- How do you create a culture of shared ownership where people don't let each other down?
- Do people regularly go above and beyond the minimum expectations?

## THE REST OF THE STORY

The two teams that were ascending Aneroid Mountain took two tacks: a risky route and a cautious one. The riskier team's leader was headstrong and felt it was best to push his team to help them realize what they were made of. The cautious leader collaborated with the team the entire time and didn't push people out of their comfort zones. Both teams encountered loose rock where the footing was unsteady, fear increased, and each fell back on their natural tendencies.

On the riskier team, the growing sense of fear, discomfort, and stress led people to harshly judge one another. They questioned each other's preparedness and ability to perform the task at hand, while others questioned teammates' compassion and leadership. Some team members wanted to trudge ahead and go it alone, but they all knew the objective was to get to the summit together. Fortunately for the cautious team, the experiences they had already gone through—hiking, cooking duties, building a shelter, solving problems—allowed them to build on the trust they needed to suspend biases and help pull everyone together through the challenge.

To everyone's surprise, both teams reached the summit at the same time. If you asked the cautious team if they'd be willing to keep going and climb another summit, they'd have said, "Heck yeah!" If you asked the riskier team the same thing, they would have said, "Ah, heck no!" But that's not to say the riskier team didn't gain something from the experience. They learned about how they all perform under stress and began to recognize the strengths and weaknesses of the team, and each other. In the end, neither team failed, and they both made it to the summit safely with new knowledge about themselves as individuals, who's who, and how their different roles cultivate the group dynamic.

Which leader and team do you think was more effective? Which team would you want to be a member of? Personally, we believe the cautious team won out, and for one primary reason: tone. They knew who was who and how each person contributed to the group dynamic. High performing leaders read the team, interpret the group strengths, and keep people focused and motivated. They play to people's strengths and, in the process, build an indomitable team.

## CONCLUSION

The benefits of a group of individuals focused more on teaming than individual pursuits are found in results, retention, and esprit de corps. When teams are adventurous, and fear is absent, they develop a tolerance for adversity and uncertainty. Dynamic teams are inclusive, constantly seeking the group's input, and they don't wait to ask for help when needed. High performing teams that truly bond are also highly protective, staying calm and focused when it comes to difficulties. Those with palpable positivity and a bias to action are driven, and they constantly ask, "For whose good do we serve?" Teams that are comprised of individuals who aspire to be authentic and selfless seek feedback to learn from the experience and tend to develop greater self-awareness.

The best teams are driven by the desire to fulfill expectations and obligations with discipline and perseverance. This sense of duty is commonly thought of as taking care of the person to your right and left. Having someone's back. Not letting the team down. They shun those who criticize, condemn, and complain. They know success comes from first being squared away so they can focus on the needs of others, rather than vice versa. In the end, the most important thing is to uphold the values of the organization. You must create an environment where purpose is clear and shared accountability is seen as a sacred duty. Letting other people down when it comes to commitments, promises, and obligations is simply not an option.

## THE THREE PILLARS

### *Leading Self*

Self-awareness is not just about knowing your proclivities. It's about knowing how your behavior affects others' feelings. Continue honing your ability to regulate your emotional response in a way that's best for the team—not a response that satisfies your own self-serving goals.

- When you last experienced a period of high stress, how would others say you showed up?
- How would you prefer to react to a stressful event in the future?
- What strengths do you have that add unique value to your team? Are there other roles you can play to add balance to the team?

### *Leading Others*

The group must understand the normal stages of team development and the roles required to allow for the yin and yang of a team and reflect diversity of thought.

- How do you help your team move quickly from storm to norm?
- How can you slow down before you enter into periods of high stress, ensuring you are applying the TREE expectations?
- What strengths do your teammates have that add unique value to the team? How can you best leverage the strengths of your teammates to add unique value to the team?

### *Leading the Organization*

Enlightened leaders create an environment of psychological safety in which they can be confident that the emerging group dynamic conforms to the values of the organization while allowing for authenticity.

- As you move toward building a high performing team, how can you ensure commitments, promises, and obligations are honored?
- How can each member help others on the team maximize their potential?
- What are the ways you can ensure the friction you experience results in traction versus drag and drama?

CHAPTER 8

# OBSTACLES

## *Expecting Adversity*

> "If we went out as individuals, not everyone would have made it to the top. Because we went out as a team, and approached it as a team, we all made it."
>
> —*Dave Scott, Executive Participant, Ouray, Colorado*

Imagine the towering sandstone towers and slot canyons of Utah. With blue skies, hot days, cool nights, and rugged terrain, Moab consistently delivers jaw-dropping sunrises and sunsets, some of the best in all of the western United States. Mary, a participant on the Crucible Expedition, was a top executive with a large, multinational corporation. She was the sort of person more comfortable in high heels than hiking boots, but she was out there fully committed to the experience, looking for a digital detox as a respite from her pressure-cooker job.

It was the second day of the trek, and her team needed to ascend a steep spur. To visualize a spur, put your hand out, extend your fingers apart from each other, and then make a claw. Each finger is basically a spur, and the space in between is what's called a draw. The sides of a spur can be steep, and the terrain in the Utah desert is rocky and sandy, making the footing rather slippery. It was on one of these spurs that Mary stopped the group and said, "If I fall right here, I will die." She looked around, panic in her eyes. Then she caught her breath and declared, "I'm done. I am not going up there. Let's figure out an alternative." One of the Crucible rules is that if you think something is unsafe, say something. And she sure did! No one argued with her.

Looking at what happened from a different perspective, another participant recalled, "We got to one part of a traverse and Mary was not comfortable with the movement. It was a windy, cold part of the day, near dusk. We put in a rope to get across one part and we were about to do it and she said, 'No, we do not need to go any further.' As a team, we all supported her decision and went back to camp. I remember it being a nonissue. It was handled perfectly. At the end of the day, no one felt like they let anyone down, and nobody overreacted."

Before executing the alternative plan and route, the leader said to Mary, "I get it—this is really scary to you. And the risk is very visible. What about the times you ask people on your team to do things, and they're scared to death, but you think it's no big deal because the risk isn't physical?" Mary looked down for a minute, and then said, "You're right. I bet I ask people to leave their comfort zone all the time without thinking it over." The group talked a little more about Mary's comfort level with her perceived risk, and they agreed to change the route. But everyone was amazed and impressed at how Mary's confidence allowed her to speak up and show vulnerability. And like a self-perpetuating motion machine, her vulnerability seemed to give her even more confidence to speak up and be honest with herself and the team.

High performing teams are willing to take risks and adapt. They're willing to attempt something—and not succeed. But note, "not succeeding" and "failure" are miles apart. As discussed in chapter seven, abject failure only occurs if no lesson was learned. The goal is to achieve a balance between helping your team leave their comfort zone so they know how far they can go, but not go so far that it breaks their spirit. This balance can be delicate, but when a team is willing and courageous enough to push themselves, they can learn their true capabilities and face obstacles unabated. Big goals always require an adventurous degree of discomfort, sacrifice, and self-discipline.

Encountering obstacles is inevitable. You need to let your team know adversity is to be expected. But just muscling through adversity is not enough. You must have the courage to know when to reassess, move past your pride, and speak truth to power. As a group, by questioning whether your actions will move the team toward the desired end state, each person (and the team as a whole) has a better chance of actually getting there. The inability to complete a short-term goal does not mean you won't be able to get beyond any given obstacle for the bigger goals. You might just have to find another way around—or through.

To do so, you must cultivate grit to amplify action, developing the resilience to meet obstacles and boldly move you toward your audacious goals. This resilience will prepare you for the inevitable obstacles, setbacks, issues, problems, and challenges that we call adversity. Such preparation creates an environment that lends itself to a positive attitude among team members no matter the circumstances. The focus is on moving forward, getting beyond the low points, and preparing for the next challenge ahead. And it all starts with recognizing the next challenge out there waiting for you, right around the next corner.

## DIFFICULT TIMES

In the military, the first order of business is to always be aware of the situation. It's called situational awareness, and it's akin to hyper-vigilance—there is always a need for contingency planning. It hearkens back to the adage that "no plan survives first contact with the enemy," because in complex environments there is always unpredictability. VUCA[1] is a term that was coined by the U.S. Army War College in the 1980s to describe the volatile, uncertain, complex, and ambiguous geopolitical landscape that emerged after the end of the Cold War. It was brought into the business world by economists and university professors Warren Bennis and Burt Nanus in their book, *Leaders: The Strategies for Taking Charge.*

Why VUCA? Aren't they just four words with essentially the same meaning? Not quite. A volatile environment is one in which the nature and speed of change forces action, while uncertainty alludes to a lack of predictability and understanding. Complexity creates confusion through no clear cause and effect due to the multiple forces impacting the environment, and ambiguity is a fog that further confuses cause and effect through misunderstandings and mixed messages.

The reality is that our world has become a lot more VUCA since the 1980s. Leaders who expect certainty and clarity will find themselves ill-prepared to face the ever-present change, confusion, and challenges that typify the twenty-first century. Nature paints this picture vividly, especially in slot canyons. The weather can change in a moment, creating flash-flood risks, for example, which will affect the planned journey (volatility). A sudden teammate injury can throw a wrench in the mission (uncertainty). Inefficient forward movement because of delays or a misinterpretation of the map creates layers of confusion (complexity). And interpersonal challenges through miscommunication and misunderstanding can throw even the best team for a loop (ambiguity).

How you deal with VUCA on the side of a physical obstacle, like a spur, is similar to how you work through it in the office environment. When teams find themselves struggling with volatility, they need to re-anchor on the initial vision. This grounding prepares them to anticipate and adapt when circumstances get hairy. In times of uncertainty, teammates must increase their understanding of the situation through genuine curiosity. Complexity needs clarity. Ask yourself, "Where can I eliminate confusion by being crystal clear, even in small ways?" Clarity also helps to diminish ambiguity. But even if you ease the tension of these environmental pressures, adversity is still bound to arise.

The question, then, is, How will you respond to problems, challenges, setbacks, disappointments, and criticism? One way is to demonstrate agility. Agile teams encourage participation through debate and dissent, and a willingness to move outside of comfort zones. They possess the grit required to push further as they gain experience and knowledge. They also have a sense of collective "stick-to-it-iveness" to see a task or goal through and put the needs of the whole team ahead of their own individual discomfort. This type of grit and discipline manifests itself in doing more even when you're tired because you'd rather be exhausted than let your team down and risk not accomplishing the goal.

We rarely look over the side of a literal cliff that may result in death with one wrong move, but figuratively, we may often feel this way. The VUCA environment we face today means that the decisions we make have increasingly high-stakes outcomes for ourselves, as well as our teams, who entrust us with their livelihood.

## PERCEPTIONS

As shown in the opening story of this chapter, risk is extremely relative and perceptions vary, depending on the lens you use to observe your surroundings. Change the lens, change your perspective, along with your assumptions, beliefs, and even expectations. What Mary thought was a treacherous risk, another participant thought was "no big deal." We all have fears and insecurities, but they're not all the same, because we're not all the same. Everyone feels and displays fear differently. An indomitable team knows each other's strengths and weaknesses, but what distinguishes them is that their relationships are so tight they can communicate without even speaking. They are able to recognize that though their perceptions might be different, they are there for each other when a team member is unsure, tepid, scared, or fearful.

Remember Bill from chapter two, the middle-aged executive with the heavy 1970s frame backpack? What was right for him at that moment was swapping backpacks with his team member Angie, but that might not have been the best option for another person. Contrast his experience with that of Renee, on a Crucible in western Colorado. Renee was struggling—panicking, really. Her teammates recognized what was going on despite her normally calm and driven personality, and they wanted to reassure her and ensure their collective success. One teammate, Tom, asked to take her backpack during a difficult stretch of the trail. He knew he had the stamina to support her in this moment and that it could make a difference in her attitude and outlook. She declined. Then another teammate encouraged Renee to let Tom take her backpack. She declined again. Renee knew that in order to continue building her resilience for the long-term success of the team, she needed to complete the challenge on her own. Here is Renee's perspective, through her lens:

> *We were way back in there, and hadn't seen another hiker in twenty-four hours. We were in a deep canyon and had to go straight down the side, cross the dry canyon, and go back up the other side. I was the leader for the day and I got to the top of the edge and completely panicked. I was trying to figure out how to say, "I don't think I can do this; I need someone else to lead for a while" without looking like a coward as the only woman; and I didn't need to say anything, because someone else noticed my face. That person asked to take my pack and I declined. Someone else said, "Why don't you let him take your pack?" I needed time to get through it on my own. The guide helped me every step, but I didn't even begin negotiating the tricky obstacle until the team was already through. I remember sobbing on the other side of the obstacle, but everyone was cheering for me. This was my company's*

*internal Crucible and I felt like I had a lot to prove because of my gender. Sometimes in business and in life, that matters.*

The weight of the backpack was not actually Renee's problem; it was how her teammates thought they could best help her. But recognizing her determination to get through the challenge herself, they stepped back and patiently encouraged her. She needed to tackle the challenge on her own, and in doing so, she turned it into a growth opportunity. Renee was able to reframe the risks she encountered, instead of drowning in doubt and fear. She still tells this story years later, and how much the experience meant to her. More importantly, after that Crucible, she began changing her narrative on everyday challenges and obstacles, which she believes has caused her to become a more confident leader.

How we view a situation, and how stress manifests in each of us, shapes the way in which we respond. Do we see the situation as a threat, or an opportunity? Are we excited about the possibilities, or paralyzed by the risks? Stephen Covey, author of the longtime bestseller *The 7 Habits of Highly Effective People*, has helped countless readers recognize that we must seek first to understand, then to be understood. Just as Renee's team came to better understand her on the edge of that arroyo, once you truly understand your employees, your team, and your people, you are best positioned to be understood in return. To activate your team through difficulties, you have to first see reality from their point of view, recognizing how their perceptions play into the decisions they make and how you can best influence others. Ask yourself:

1. Can you see the obstacles from your employees' perspective?
2. Do you understand all of the forces at play that motivate, or demotivate?
3. What can you do to bring out the best in people?

You need to ask your employees questions to understand their perceptions and points of view. Their values, assumptions, expectations, beliefs, and perspectives can't be observed like behaviors, but inquiry allows you to infer the causal effects between what you see (your perception) and what it means (informed action).

Try, for example, asking your team thought-provoking questions. These can be as simple as, "What part of your responsibilities are you avoiding right now? Why?" "What is the area that, if you made an improvement, you and others would see the greatest return on time, energy, and dollars invested?" Thoughtful questions help you gain insight and develop empathy, and they are the key to unlocking behaviors that generate results.

You must then take the initiative to use what you've learned from your people to influence change. Initiative is infectious, and it can be the catalyst for creating an environment where your team has the confidence to be proactive as well. If you use different lenses to understand your team's point of view, you will have a better chance for them to see what you see—and what they could be. By recognizing your employees' perceptions, you can intentionally create a culture where they are emboldened to demonstrate initiative in their everyday actions. That's where you want to be. That's where you need to be.

## MINDSET

When teams encounter obstacles and adversity, the leader's common rallying cry is, "We need to be more innovative!" That leader might also ask their team to be more strategic, or proactive, or to act like owners. No matter the exact words, what that leader is actually looking for in the development of new products, or novel efficiencies, is a mindset that is part of a culture for learning and growth. Identifying, adopting, and spreading a growth mindset throughout the organization will make an enormous impact on objectives and outcomes.

When you hit obstacles and face adversity, the key indicator on how you will think, and what you will do, starts with your mindset.

Fortunately, we can rely on the work of Dr. Carol Dweck, American psychologist and a professor at Stanford University. Through her research, Dweck shows that a growth mindset, versus a fixed mindset, is the key to overcoming struggles, difficulties, challenges, and problems. In short, the right mindset better helps us handle adversity.

In a fixed mindset, people believe their basic intelligence or talents are fixed traits. Because they believe their identity is locked, they purposely validate that perception through their actions. When people with fixed mindsets fail at something, they tend to tell themselves they can't or won't be able to do it. And because they tell themselves so, they don't, which is much different than can't. You can identify these team members by the following:

- They avoid difficulties and challenges.
- They may give up quickly and blame themselves for not succeeding.
- They display pessimistic attitudes, and you may hear them make statements like, "This is pointless."

In a growth mindset, people believe their basic abilities can be developed through dedication and hard work. This view nurtures curiosity and resilience and helps people not only face obstacles, but seek them.[2] The growth mindset can be seen in team members who take the following actions:

- Embrace difficulties as a challenge and see the possibilities that come from persistence.
- Demonstrate perseverance and aren't too hard on the person in the mirror.
- Learn from setbacks and view the effort as part of the journey.

People who embrace growth mindsets learn faster and view setbacks as opportunities to improve and flourish. Renee, mentioned earlier in this chapter, demonstrated a growth mindset when she pushed through her fears and doubts to conquer the obstacle in her path. If she had stayed in a fixed mindset, she might have turned back or allowed her teammates to make the process as easy as possible. As a result, she would have learned less and lost some of her own agency for future growth.

The impact of her growth mindset also extended beyond herself, positively impacting her team—and their perception of her. It is impossible to watch others embrace difficulties with gusto, or demonstrate perseverance, without being motivated to act in a similar fashion. Growth begets growth. A growth mindset is not a personality trait. As Dweck explains, it is a choice that can be learned,[3] and as the leader, you can help create an environment in which this mindset plays a major role as a catalyst for innovation.

So how do you build such a culture? Create a constructive climate where you'll actually hear about difficulties—or to "help bad news travel fast." Reinforce positivity so difficulties aren't disguised as complaints, criticisms, and overall condemnation (the three Cs mentioned in chapter six). We all migrate to our comfort zones, so you sometimes have to steer people in a different direction to help them develop new habits. To leave our comfort zone, we must carve out time to work on things that are long-term important, but not always short-term urgent.

Our professional development will never be urgent per se, but it will always be vitally important to being a successful leader. There will be constant distractions, and the latest fire to put out, but leaders must take time for themselves to hone their craft, including skills like self-awareness, empathy, listening, asking great questions, and handling difficult conversations. Help people say no to things they're comfortable doing but are not necessarily growth producing, and embrace challenges in areas where there is low knowledge, skill, or expertise.

As the leader, the environment has to be forgiving and safe to try new things, but you must still say no to things, otherwise people are going to revert back to old habits. Think *bouncebackability*. This term was coined by Tom Peters, the author of *In Search of Excellence: Lessons from America's Best-Run Companies*. Bouncebackability develops best through trial—and lots of error—and is a necessary trait you want your team members to possess so they can bounce back from setbacks.

## GRIT

Grit is an act and a form of courage, because it represents resolve and guarantees strength of character. Like leadership, grit isn't something you're born with. The ability to embrace adversity is refined over time through tough experiences. Grit is an ability to embrace, learn from, and overcome inevitable difficulties. Not everyone has grit. But everyone is capable of *developing* grit. It starts with ownership of your actions, a personal responsibility to lead one's self. You need it most when you're up against obstacles, challenges, and problems, as it is the most effective way to embrace adversity and emerge knowing you did your very best. With that in mind, we define grit as the amalgamation of three traits:

**Grit =**
**Passion (purpose) + Determination (will) + Persistence (stamina)**

With hard work and discipline, these traits can be become productive habits:

- **Passion.** Passion leads you to fulfill your purpose by putting the time and effort needed into developing the skills and acquiring the experience necessary to be competent in your job, position, or field. That's the minimum. Gritty leaders are curious. They set aside time to learn, to discover new ideas and understand what's happening in the world around them. They read voraciously, listen to podcasts, take online courses, work with coaches, and pursue other means to continue their professional development. The investment in learning takes sacrifice, because acquiring knowledge happens at the expense of something else. You may feel that you could better spend your time "working" than reading the news that morning, but in reality, part of your work as a leader is staying informed and intellectually sharp.

- **Determination.** Determination is about approaching goals with a firmness of purpose and a resoluteness. In part, it relies on the ability to regulate your emotions in a way that delivers a response that's best for the team. It takes self-discipline to make a decision and set a course that may, at times, be arduous. Determination creates and sustains the momentum required for overcoming friction when tackling big goals.
- **Persistence.** Persistence is about the ability to maintain attention and focus for the long haul. It's tenacity. The vision and direction that passion and determination instill in an effort must then be met with fierce resolve in spite of the obstacles encountered. Even with setbacks, it is essential to remain committed and optimistic to get others to do the same. As Calvin Coolidge famously said, "Nothing in this world can take the place of persistence. Talent will not: nothing is more common than unsuccessful men with talent. Genius will not; unrewarded genius is almost a proverb. Education will not: the world is full of educated derelicts. Persistence and determination alone are omnipotent."[4]

All three of these habits can be developed by creating "white space" in your life, a dedicated time and place for you to think, reflect, reenergize, and refocus your efforts. White space also allows you to look for the root cause of issues, not just the effects, and to weigh options, plan for contingencies, decide the criteria and process for how you will make decisions, and craft messages that inspire people to full commitment versus mere compliance.

It's important that you model gritty habits so you can encourage them in others, especially in the challenging moments that so often characterize our everyday lives. A great example was on a Crucible when the leader for the day, Dave, saw Clint's grit wavering, and he knew he had to help. Here's how he explained what happened:

> *Clint is an emotional and caring person. He is a lot more capable and courageous than he gives himself credit for. He was in his head and making the climb a bigger deal than it really was. I didn't want his fear and negativity polluting the rest of the group as it would take away the joy of the climb. I asked myself, "How can we make the most of this experience?" I said to Clint, "Look at how far you've already gone. Think how you're going to feel when you accomplish this." I think I helped him enjoy the journey along the way—reveling in his mini-accomplishments by focusing on one step at a time. It's funny, going through that challenge with him made it all that much more joyful for me. It was almost a godsend because it got me out of my head as I grasped the gift of helping someone else. When you're going through turbulence and fear, the gift of helping someone else distracts you from your own head trash.*

Dave called on his passion to help increase both his and Clint's grit. By focusing on serving a teammate, the climb's journey took on a different purpose. And now Dave could not let Clint down. That was enough for him to dig deep, refocus his determination, and persist through the strain. Dave amplified his own grit by praising what had already been accomplished, allowing Clint to see the progress of each step.

If you're willing to embrace new habits, you can cultivate grit in the face of adversity to learn, grow, adapt, overcome challenges, and inspire others to accomplish truly heroic aspirations. Some companies like 3M and Gore are famous for announcing and rewarding failures because they represent courage, risk, vulnerability, learning, and a way forward for the next success. Embracing adversity isn't easy, because it also means facing the possibility of failure. Yet, you must create the opportunity to step back and see the gap between where you are and where you want to be.

When failures happen, look at them as an opportunity to explore different options, perspectives, and assumptions, and then try multiple alternatives. Have your team walk you through a debrief of what went well, what could have been better, and their collective recommendations and actions for future success. When your team embraces grit, they'll innovate their way out of innumerable difficulties. American businessman Robert Kiyosaki summed it up best: "Losers quit when they fail. Winners fail until they succeed."

## RESILIENCE

Resilient leaders have an ownership mentality, which means they assume complete responsibility for their behavior, decisions, and outcomes. They approach challenges with a sense of self-reliance, and as an opportunity to show initiative, assume control, and lead their team with an unrelenting focus on the overarching goal. Soldiers who go through special operations training have a unique way of creating an ownership mentality that turns adversity into opportunity. In a wry way, they say pain is weakness leaving your body. Suffering is inevitable, and how we deal with it can be an indication, or aptitude, for how we handle difficulties. The way people candidly chide one another can be indicators of a team's ability to bounce back from difficulties with resilience. During military training, you're likely to hear:

"Suck it up, buttercup!"
"Can you believe we get paid to do this stuff?"
"I wish it would rain harder!"

What do you hear from your team during challenges, crises, and uncertainty? When you trust your team, and they trust you and each other, they align to embrace challenges with resilience and a sense of control. Stanford psychologist Philip Zimbardo said, "A locus of control orientation is a belief about whether the outcomes of our actions are contingent on what we do (internal control orientation), or on events outside our personal control (external control orientation)."[5] We can dwell on the negative, or we can be resilient. Resilience allows us to readily return to original form after an adverse event. Tapping into your own self-reliance means using the inevitable adversity we all face to continuously improve so we can take on the next challenge with even more passion, persistence, and determination.

The one thing we have absolute control over is how we respond to our environment, so it makes sense that optimists tap into their own self-reliance whereas pessimists can often flounder in learned helplessness. If you see members of your team looking at adverse situations as permanent, pervasive, or personal, you have someone who is exhibiting pessimistic tendencies. Take the optimistic approach, and help them see the difficult times as temporary, limited, and external.

**PRO TIP**

If you expect adversity, then you need vigilance. As we say on the Crucible, if it's not safe, say something. The last thing a leader needs when facing obstacles is silence. Silence can mean people are afraid to speak, which means an element of fear exists. When there is an absence of fear, there is trust, and people will speak up and ask the needed and tough questions. No healthy conflict, no real commitment. No commitment, no accountability. No accountability, no results. To face obstacles and tackle inevitable difficulties, make sure you're creating a climate where people feel safe to ask questions, disagree, debate, and deliberate. When they do, they will also be helping you gain perspective by seeing the obstacles early enough to take corrective action.

Now take a moment to consider your own organization and how you approach obstacles:

- How can you help others with the part of obstacles that is within your control, or within your ability, to influence?
- Are you asking thought-provoking questions to truly understand others' points of view, or are you running roughshod over people?
- Are you using inevitable setbacks as case studies for growth, development, and continuous improvement to make your team better, stronger, and ultimately more fulfilled?

## THE REST OF THE STORY

Everyone was concerned that Mary's action on that spur, and the subsequent inability of the team to "accomplish the mission," would impact the whole expedition. But sometimes, when an action is left incomplete, that's when the real learning takes place. Because the team was open to understanding Mary's viewpoint, and demonstrated a growth mindset, the team took away a new understanding of what can be gained when balancing risk and reward. This wasn't a profit and loss or a business growth chart; this was real, primal, and they could feel it in their bones.

Ultimately, the team was aligned around their ground rules to support one another and allow people to speak their truth. Because they knew Mary had reached her limit of acceptable risk, the team wasn't resentful that they didn't make it to the planned base camp destination. Her decision was supported, and the whole situation ultimately became a nonissue. If Mary had been met with frustration and criticism, the likelihood that others would have spoken up in the future would have been greatly diminished.

For Mary, it was a moment of balancing risk and reward. One of her insights was, "In an environment where I was completely uncomfortable, with no expertise, I showed up exactly as I do in the corporate world. When the juice isn't worth the squeeze, I stop. If we aren't achieving what we want, I ask whether it's worth it. All three special operations guys thanked me for calling it." At the end of the day, with a glorious sunset as a backdrop, nobody overreacted and Mary did not feel as though she let anyone down. Her teammates' reaction made it clear they were no longer just *working* as a team; they had *become* a team. Undeterred, they had the determination and persistence needed to tackle the next day, and the next obstacle, with a newfound sense of purpose of what it means to handle adversity.

## CONCLUSION

Managing through obstacles can try the best of leaders, but adversity can also be a tool for exponential learning and growth, as well as a bonding experience that can strengthen your team. Whether the difficult times are thrust upon you or internally created, becoming the beacon for hope and inspiration is a duty and responsibility you've assumed as a leader. You need to continue to inspire your people by effectively engaging them at a deep level.

To enhance your team's ability to fully participate, even when times are tough, ensure that you're seeing the obstacles through multiple lenses. It's easy to be reactive during difficult times, but it takes a steady hand to properly diagnose the root cause of the obstacle and apply the right leadership lever in the right way at the right time. Stay curious. If you approach the challenge with a mindset targeted toward growth instead of failure, you unlock an array of possibilities. Cultivate your habits of grit by driving your purpose with determination and persistence. Buried in the setbacks and hard times are the seeds of future victories if you take the time to step back, reset, refocus, and reenergize your team.

## THE THREE PILLARS

### *Leading Self*

Assume ownership for your area of responsibility with grit and discipline. Team members have to trust you are going to do the right thing. At times, being true to yourself takes courage, especially when you have a point of view different from others.

- What are you leaving unsaid that, if you said it, would help your team understand your perspective?
- What are the obstacles, challenges, and problems you can reframe as opportunities?
- In what situations are you more likely to have a fixed mindset, and what do you need to do to have a growth mindset?

### *Leading Others*

By demonstrating ownership you will instill a sense of duty in your team. You can boost ownership in others by getting people to not only work with each other, but work *for* each other.

- Which challenges need reframing in order to foster curiosity and growth from teammates?
- In what ways have you seen your team demonstrate responsibility for each other, and how can you amplify a greater sense of caring?
- What would be a meaningful way to enhance your team's level of resilience today?

### *Leading the Organization*

Align team members and conduct courageous conversations that result in greater collaboration, understanding, and focus.

- How can you use the challenges your team is facing as a bonding experience?
- How can you create clarity for your organization in light of inevitable and constant uncertainty?
- How do you know when it's the right time to step back, reset, refocus, and reenergize your team?

CHAPTER 9

# RHYTHM

## *Creating Synergy*

> "It was the investment in people and knowing their strengths and aspirations that allowed us to find where we fit, and where we could add unique value to move the team forward."
>
> —*Jim Vaselopulos, Executive Participant, Patagonia*

Sal, a junior executive in a global manufacturing company with over 15,000 employees, was the leader for the last day in Moab, tasked with taking the team all the way back to the trailhead, where civilization awaited. Considering everything he had learned about the team collectively, and each of his teammates individually, he briefed them on the route, weather, terrain, expected pace, and destination. But as he explained the plan for the day, he got the feeling the team was only half listening. He thought to himself, *It's the last day; everyone is ready to get back, get a good meal, and a hot shower. Of course they're preoccupied.* With this assumption rattling in his head, he lowered his expectations, but kept his high-energy approach and plan in place.

Once they started hiking, however, he was in for a surprise. Along the route, team members talked among themselves, some telling jokes and laughing, others in deep one-on-one conversations. But no one discussed the movement forward, and no one seemed to be paying particular attention to his approach. However, the way they got across the streams, navigated ledges, and ended breaks without anyone saying a word all showed Sal he had nothing to worry about—they were one team, acting in near unison. They had found their rhythm—whether he was actively leading or not.

Once a rhythm is established, it will only stay intact with diligent care and concern from all the team members. Challenges arise and decisions and changes must be made to accommodate the reality on the ground. The key for the team is to continue pushing one another toward achieving the desired goal, while also keeping spirits high, and making sure everyone is physically safe and mentally sound. If the rhythm flounders, movement forward must be corrected. By clearly defining expectations, and helping people fall into a comfortable rhythm of communication and collaboration, the team avoids the difficulties that accompany unpredictable situations and changing priorities.

You can sense rhythm on a team when everyone completes tasks with minimal communication; when expectations about direction, pace, and tone are so well aligned there's an ease and efficiency in how they're approached. There is also absolute clarity on where, what, and why, and the evolved team's rhythm makes the "how" feel effortless. This is when a group truly starts performing as a team, realizing they have entered a world where they're dealing with "good problems to have," the sort that results from abundance versus scarcity, like growth from increased volume, demand, and new offerings.

Cultivating a sustainable rhythm is not a solitary task; the entire team must be aligned to achieve success. Effective leadership demands a combination of vision, conviction, and discipline, along with efficiency and adaptability, because the ability to pivot is crucial when difficulties are encountered. And disruptions are guaranteed to occur. A disrupted rhythm can have significant consequences, as it can cause a rapid decline in team engagement and performance. It's therefore essential to foster and design an environment that enhances team members' ability to identify and respond to each other's needs, enabling them to develop a duty to one another and a natural rhythm that propels the team toward success together.

## RHYTHM AS FLOW

Rhythm can be defined as a strong, regular, repeated pattern of movement. It's like the instant you hear the drumbeat at the start of your favorite song and you're almost involuntarily compelled to start moving some part of your body, be it your thumbs on the dashboard or your hips on the dance floor. It's your heart engaging your hands, or your feet, or both! A team rhythm aims to do the same—compel you, almost involuntarily, to act and move in a powerful way in sync with your teammates.

Rhythm can be thought of as a state of flow among team members. The concept of flow was first described by Hungarian psychologist and professor Mihály Csíkszentmihályi as a state of mind where an individual is so intensely focused that everything around them—all other distractions—is completely blocked out. Flow is so profound and intense that a person feels one with the work or activity they are performing. If you're a musician, it might be while playing a piece you've practiced time and again. Or if you're a writer, it might be when you find yourself on a roll in the middle of a chapter. As a business leader, you might enter a flow state when you're preparing for a speech, becoming so involved in the message you want to convey and with such ease that you completely lose track of time.

For teams, flow leads to the ability to communicate without words and a sense of near bliss in working with each other. It's a feeling of safety, satisfaction, a sense of duty to others, and profound pride in seeing the team succeed, despite struggles and setbacks. It could even be considered love, as in a deep caring for the people on your team.

Throughout the Crucible, team members quickly start to learn each other's strengths and weaknesses. In time, they fall in sync and develop a rhythm. Communication happens almost telepathically. Efficiencies are realized. It becomes clear who needs to reduce the weight in their pack when the group is climbing, or who needs to be placed in the front of the group so the team doesn't experience the dreaded accordion effect, in which people in the back fall behind, then have to move faster to catch up. The same happens on a highly functioning business team. People put in the hours to hit a deadline without being asked. Team members check in on each other after a meeting, even after observing something as subtle as a furrowed brow. The team decides when to celebrate and let their hair down the same way they know when to buckle down when the pressure is on.

The famous composer George Gershwin wrote "I Got Rhythm," and if you know the tune, it's hard not to hear it in your head as you recall the lyrics. A fine-tuned team works the same way, its rhythm like a song stuck in your head—it feels easy, natural, and comfortable. The most effective teams collectively possess key traits that produce an indomitable rhythm for the team. Some of these traits have been touched on earlier in the book, but here they are geared toward that strong, regular, repeated pattern of movement that results in a state of team flow.

### *Clarity*

Clear expectations create the driving drumbeat for a team's rhythm, providing answers to the following questions:

- **What Is Our Shared Vision?** Knowing *where* you're headed is critical if you're to make sound operational and strategic decisions about what the company will or will not do, or where you will or will not serve. For example, LinkedIn's vision is to "create economic opportunity for every member of the global workforce."[1] Google looks to "provide access to the world's information in one click."[2] And Patagonia's vision states, "We're in business to save our home planet."[3] Note that each company focuses not just on the immediate country or region around them but the *entire* world: "global," "world," and "planet." That type of audacious vision has been a large part of these three companies' success.
- **What Is Our Shared Mission?** Understanding what to do, and why to do it, is key. A mission statement can help facilitate that understanding by clearly describing *what* your organization does in pursuit of its vision. For example, LinkedIn's stated mission is to "connect the world's professionals to make them more productive and successful."[4] Google's is, "Organize the world's information and make it universally accessible and useful."[5] And Patagonia aims to "build the best product, cause no unnecessary harm, use business to inspire and implement solutions to the environmental crisis."[6] While all three of these mission statements explain how the companies will accomplish their vision, they are also broad enough to allow for the flexibility to adapt, evolve, and innovate as the external environment changes.
- **What Are Our Shared Values?** Values describe *how* you will fulfill your vision and perform the mission. They explain what the company holds dear as key traits and behaviors required for effective teamwork and individual performance. A common starting point for many organizations is to establish how

individuals will behave, which may include one of the following traits: creative, customer-focused, respectful, team-oriented, compassionate, driven, bold, curious, competitive, inclusive, and selfless.

Providing clarity to the big picture and setting standards for performance underscores all other aspects of a team moving forward with rhythm. Once the team knows *where* they're going (vision), *what* they're doing (mission), and *how* they're doing it (values), all they need is to behave in ways that produce results, as typified by the traits outlined below.

### *Standards*

If the mission, vision, and values are the rhythm, then the standards are the cadence. Standards are upheld when specific observable behaviors, tied to an organization's values, lead to operational excellence, high engagement, and overall productivity. When standards aren't upheld, quality, morale, and performance fall apart. Behaviors all have a yin and a yang, and the best leaders exercise judgment to know when to emphasize a strength and when to dial it back. In other words, sometimes our dominant attributes serve us, and sometimes they get in the way of our ability to influence others.

Let's dig a little deeper into the attributes of being selfless, bold, and driven. These three attributes should sound familiar, as they are the criteria for selecting participants for Crucible Expeditions, as discussed in chapter one. Observable behaviors for those three attributes in a business setting could include helping out on a project you don't own to ensure a deadline is met, speaking up in a meeting to offer a contrarian point of view, or following up on leads despite hitting your quota early. Meeting standards makes for strong individuals, but when those individuals come together collectively in a team, they help create a strong rhythm, one that is both steady enough to maintain direction, pace, and tone, but fluid enough to adapt given new circumstances.

## Selfless

Being selfless infers a *feel-it-in-your-bones* obligation to do what's best for the team. It's a profound sense of duty to others. It's about putting the team first. A moral obligation. A responsibility. A requirement to perform a task. Effective leaders make hard choices, even if that means causing some personal discomfort. Selfless leaders feel duty-bound to serve the greater good, which often means an uncommon discipline for delayed gratification.

Competence and connection are two main components that create rhythm by which people work selflessly, and with a sense of duty. When a team trusts in each other's competence to complete the task at hand, on time, and to the agreed-upon quality standard, they naturally click. Leaders help make these connections possible by fulfilling their role and responsibility to support team members at different places on the continuum of skills, experience, and knowledge.

To help build competence among the team, leaders must gain an understanding of each individual's strengths to best frame expectations. When leaders begin to see the gaps between team members' capabilities and expectations, they can provide the development, coaching, or resources required to close those gaps. They must also keep sight of the need to build the connection between each individual on the team to solidify selflessness.

Relationships take time, and there is no substitute for getting to know and understand other people. To foster selfless behaviors, ensure there is social cohesion via real human-to-human connections. Create an environment where team members get to actually know one another. This might be through a well-thought-out icebreaker, or some other activity where people are given time to bond. This means occasionally slowing down the pace and allowing for banter, even if it might feel like a waste of time. In 2023, the surgeon general raised the alarm of the devastating impact, and public health crisis, of loneliness, isolation, and lack of connection in the United States.[7] Happiness and job satisfaction are tied to healthy social connections, and higher performance individually and collectively. When team relationships are solid, everyone has a voice, allowing them to speak up, whether to disagree, to contribute, or most importantly, to be heard. Remember, a lack of healthy and productive conflict leads to either complacency or, worse yet, fear.

## Bold

We're bold because we want to know. We're bold because we want to influence the outcome. We're bold because we're confident. Boldness and curiosity go hand in hand. The acclaimed American author, anthropologist, and filmmaker Zora Neale Hurston said of curiosity, "It is poking and prying with a purpose." Wisdom in any circumstance is highly valued, and curiosity is the prerequisite for learning and knowledge. We can see inquisitiveness through asking questions and displaying boldness. Being bold and adventurous means you are *willing to take risks.* It's not necessarily taking physical risks, but being bold in saying what you think, offering a contrarian point of view, or calling out a flaw or defect in a process.

Research shows that constraints improve people's ability to be bold and innovative, to tinker, experiment, and learn. For example, Stephan Aarstol, the author of *The Five Hour Workday: Live Differently, Unlock Productivity, and Find Happiness,* saw more focus, creativity, and productivity from his team when he introduced a time constraint—the five-hour workday versus eight-hour workday. Shortening the day might not be in the cards for your team, but consider what constraints you might be able to introduce, such as setting an aggressive deadline or applying a restrictive resource constraint, to enhance your team members' boldness.

### Driven

Drive, often described as "intrinsic motivation," is the precursor for any achievement. It's what allows people to take personal responsibility, be self-reliant, and assume ownership, without blinding ambition or sacrificing morals, principles, and ethical boundaries. Being driven is about *possessing heroic aspirations*, those that go beyond power, money, and status. An indomitable team is driven—collectively and individually—to be extraordinary, not merely excellent; and it takes dynamic teamwork. Drive is at the heart of rhythm.

A collection of people with drive is the prerequisite for creating a team with heroic aspirations, a collection of souls who truly want to make a difference in the lives of others. But that drive has to be focused to create a cadence, one in which team goals override individual ambition. Everyone can't be a soloist! When we adhere to the three attributes of being selfless, bold, and driven, we create an environment where the team feels safe, and where the collective rhythm is firmly established. This environment allows rhythm to flourish and be felt just as surely as the beat of a big bass drum.

### *Planning and Adaptability*

Intentionally setting the rhythm—that state of flow between team members—enables adaptability and supports commitment through unspoken communication and autonomous collaboration. Continuous planning and adaptation requires awareness, discipline, and a focus on execution. Think of an orchestra. Each musician knows when to play their part because they've had the discipline to rehearse on their own and follow the musical score. More importantly, the last thing they want is to let their fellow musicians down. Great orchestras don't just play with each other—they play for each other.

In order to truly focus and create alignment across the organization, prioritization is needed, and it must be heeded. By assigning more value to certain activities and tasks than others, you can develop a workable execution plan. Prioritization also requires subtraction—taking beloved items *off* the to-do list. Oftentimes, we need to say no to activities, obligations, and people we care about, and our attention needs to focus on what will provide the greatest return on time, energy, and resources.

A steady rhythm in planning also leads to growth. With that in mind, consider what individual capabilities you need to start developing in your people and on your teams now. This prioritization requires a balancing act, because it often feels as if there is no time to spend developing future capabilities due to pressing issues, deadlines, and requests. Again, rhythm cannot be established unless you have the discipline to carve out time, and hold that time as sacred. But in doing so, you are able to develop skills, knowledge, and capabilities that will be at the ready when required in the future.

### *Culture and Conviction*

The most successful organizations create a culture that supports the strategy and fosters values aligned with behaviors. Creating culture is another way of describing the need to design the environment, which is how people interact with one another in an efficient rhythm while accomplishing the mission. As discussed, culture is a result of careful design, not just the hope for a positive, healthy environment as a side effect. Think of a composer working on a movie score, considering the tone they want to set right from the start of the opening scene. The composer will stay with that rhythm throughout the movie, whether it's a tense scene or one of jubilation. Every note in a movie score is a variation on the underlying rhythm.

## ORGANIZATIONAL RHYTHM

The best organizations understand the interdependence of structure, process, incentives, and people, and they adjust the levers of structure, process, and incentives to create a working rhythm across the entire organization. In other words, excellent cross-functional collaboration with no silos and turf wars. As discussed throughout this book, this is where design plays a role in optimizing the organization. As a Crucible participant once pointed out, "Typical leadership talks about playing to strengths and we tend to compartmentalize into roles, but on the Crucible, we fell naturally into different positions in the order of march; nobody pointed out people's strengths, because the environment was created for people's strengths to emerge. That's what we need to do—create the environment for people to thrive as their whole selves."

The late Joseph A. "Bud" Ahearn, a former two-star Air Force general, who went on to be a prominent executive and board member (and a mentor to many), had a saying when it came to getting his people in tune with plans and objectives, and establishing an overall organizational rhythm:

**"People support what they help create."**

He illustrated his point with the following equation:

**E = Q * A**

**E** represents **E**ffectiveness

**Q** represents **Q**uality

**A** represents **A**cceptance

So, a leader lacking in humility, trying to be the smartest person in the room, might present a plan to the team that they think is a ten out of ten for Quality (e.g., **Q** = 10). Once the leader presents the plan—their idea alone—they go into "sell mode." Perhaps they get *some* Acceptance or buy-in (e.g., **A** = 5). Five times ten yields an Effectiveness of fifty.

On the other hand, a different leader could slow things down and listen to the voices of those closest to the process and customer. Based on input from others, they then adjust their "perfect" plan to a rhythm people buy into. After the input, they may feel that the Quality of the plan is now a seven out of ten (e.g., **Q** = 7). But now the Acceptance and buy-in rises to ten (e.g., **A** = 10). That means the Effectiveness when it comes to actually executing the plan is now seventy.

The closer the score is to one hundred, the stronger the rhythm. A score of fifty, due to a lack of acceptance, as noted above, would be an inferior outcome to a score of seventy, even though, in this example, the perceived quality of the plan may actually be lower. An equal weighting to both quality and acceptance is important to creating an engaged organization. Context is, however, paramount, so you'll know best if there is a need to alter the weight of quality or acceptance in order to reach an acceptable outcome for your team.

To create a shared rhythm, you have to engage your people, emotionally, socially, and practically. If you do, overall morale will be significantly improved and you will collectively be more likely to achieve the goals you set forth. There are four different components to master that will help you develop a truly tactical operating rhythm: communication, meetings, decisions, and debate. Though we discuss these elsewhere, let's take a look at each in turn through the lens of establishing a successful rhythm.

### *Communication*

When it comes to communication, it's easy to make all sorts of noise, but the team has to be clear about which instrument to use, at what times, and at what frequency. Think about how we have to be "multilingual" these days: email, SMS, social media and instant messaging platforms, voicemail, video, conference calls, phones, and good old-fashioned in-person interactions. Some of these languages are synchronous (two-way) and some are asynchronous (one-way). Which do you use during business hours? Which do you use during an off-hour crisis? Which do you use when something is urgent, difficult, or sensitive? It's very easy to *just get to work*, but if you don't set ground rules for the way you communicate, you better be prepared for misaligned expectations and resulting drama. Do yourself a favor and take the time to really talk through the who, what, when, where, and how aspects of communication with your leaders, your peers, your team, and your partners. Aligning communication expectations will be time well spent, allowing you to maintain the rhythm and keep your team and organization humming along.

### *Meetings*

Meetings can kill a team's rhythm if not approached with intentionality and a degree of discipline. That means keeping people focused, and following through on the promises and commitments made at the conclusion of each meeting. Based on lots of meeting mistakes over the years, listed below is a handy guide to help you and your team turn dreaded meetings into time well invested, and maybe even experience some moments of levity and fun in the process:

1. **Purpose.** Why are you assembling this group of people? Potential one-word answers: Direct, Organize, Delegate, Persuade, Listen, Motivate, Empower, Discuss, Learn, Teach, Advise, Coach, Mentor, Follow.
2. **Cost of the meeting.** Take each person's approximate hourly wage and multiply that by the length of the meeting. It might make you think twice about having a $1,000 meeting (e.g., five people, at $200 per hour multiplied by one hour) to discuss what color T-shirts you want for the company picnic!
3. **Cadence.** How often will this meeting occur? Making certain meetings predictable helps people plan their schedules.
4. **Where (in-person or remote)?**
    - **STSP.** Same time, same place (synchronous, in-person) for the most important and collaborative meetings.
    - **STDP.** Same time, different place (synchronous, virtual) for remote teams and hybrid environments, allowing flexibility.
    - **DTSP.** Different time, same place (asynchronous, messaging apps) for when the topic isn't urgent, and the team has the discipline to follow through and engage.
    - **DTDP.** Different time, different place (bulletin boards, newsletters, taped videos) for announcements and less urgent information for which no interaction is needed.
5. **Type.** What format will the meeting take? Type is different from purpose in that this is the way the meeting will be run. For example, the meeting should be designed for one of six broad topic areas: decision, status, people, clients, issues, or information.
6. **Agenda.** What are you doing to make the meeting interactive and collaborative? Consider the power of questions, stories, and how you can take the opportunity to recognize others while also framing broad expectations.

7. **Ground rules.** Below is an example of the sort of ground rules set before starting a Crucible Expedition, which establishes expectations:
    - *If it needs to be done—do it.*
    - *If others aren't pitching in, talk about it.*
    - *Compliment others' efforts.*
    - *Assume responsibility for learning.*
    - *Risk saying what you think.*
    - *Hold your views lightly.*
    - *If you don't understand, ask.*
    - *Enjoy the surroundings.*
    - *Maintain a sense of humor.*
    - *Help others learn and succeed.*
    - *Be kind and inclusive.*
    - *Push yourself.*
    - *Admit mistakes.*
    - *If it's not safe for the group, don't do it—and say something.*
8. **Assumptions.** Everyone should keep an eye out for when assumptions are made and not based on facts, and call out the need for clarification, especially if a decision hinges on data.
9. **Facilitator.** Designate a facilitator who ensures that the intended outcome is met (not necessarily the formal leader, or even "highest ranking" person) and that commitments are tracked. People tend to make more promises than they realize. The facilitator should also ensure the meeting starts and ends on time, and that the right amount of time is spent on each topic to be discussed. For long meetings (half-day or more) consider designating an energizer who tracks the group dynamic and helps the facilitator know when to take breaks and when to make the meeting more interactive. This person might also

be the one who keeps track of quotable quotes (i.e., quips, pithy sayings, and ideas that resonate).

10. **Recap.** For the minutes, the main thing is *who does what by when*? Also, for those not in the meeting, consider asking (and answering): *Who needs to communicate what to whom by when?*
11. **Rate meeting.** Lastly, on a scale of one to three, have every person rate the meeting by holding up one to three fingers. If people did not rate the meeting a three, ask them what would have made the meeting more effective.

Meeting discipline, structure, and transparency will keep the entire organization aligned, sow the seeds of trust, and break down silos to foster engagement and innovation. Remember, meetings are for coordination and collaboration. People should be excited for the opportunity to meaningfully connect in meetings, as compared to dread going to them. Further, effective meetings will create real accountability for team members to fulfill their commitments to each other and ensure that the organizational rhythm is sustained.

### *Decisions*

Too often, decisions can be like the can that gets kicked down the road for weeks and months on end. Decision delays hurt the team's rhythm by introducing uncertainty, doubt, and ambiguity, draining energy and morale. Such delays happen when you have not established the criteria by which your team prioritizes decisions. The criteria should align with the organization's core values. How the decision will be made must also be stated as an easy-to-follow process. When developing the criteria for how decisions are made, keep in mind, *people support what they help create.* Be deliberate about the following and communicate which path you're taking so the team knows that to expect:

- **Are the decisions autocratic?** That is, you decide and announce (which usually also means *selling* the decision to the team and key stakeholders).
- **Will the decision be collaborative?** You present the decision you're leaning toward and request feedback.
- **Are you striving for consensus?** You're asking for input and aiming to make a joint decision.
- **Do you think being democratic is the way to go?** Everyone gets a voice, and a vote. Full disclosure on this one—we have yet to hear someone make a case for this in the business world, because there is always one person who is ultimately accountable and responsible for the outcome (i.e., the proverbial buck stops with them!).

When you're clear with regard to how decisions are made—both the process and which criteria carry the most weight—your team is much more likely to get on board quickly and maintain the operational rhythm as you intend.

### *Debate*

Of the four components required to develop a tactical operating rhythm, healthy debate is one of the hardest to achieve. Too often in today's organizations, you are likely to find either unhealthy and disrespectful arguments or unhealthy niceties that lead to unproductive groupthink. When conversations get emotionally heated with a group of people—and they will—that is not the time to attempt a rational discussion about how to resolve the issue. How to create and sustain healthy conflict resolution has to be discussed before conversations go sideways, and it must be in accordance with what the organization truly values.

You can't say "we want you to fail fast and often," and then punish people for mistakes. And you can't tell people you don't like surprises and then admonish them for not delivering bad news. There has to be consistency in what is expected from the behaviors that align with core values. Take the time to talk about where problems might occur. The two most common situations are when someone does not do what they say they would and when someone is being disrespectful to another team member. Make your own list of potential situations when conversations and work could go sideways, and then discuss how unacceptable behavior will be flagged, discussed, and resolved. The teams that plan for debate and disagreement will create an efficient rhythm that better balances productivity and adaptability, and will outperform other teams by huge margins.

## PRO TIP

One of the most surprising ahas on a Crucible came in Dominguez Canyon, a pristine desert wilderness area in western Colorado. A special operations commando was sharing a perspective with an executive, and simply said, "A commander's intent is about the *what* and the *why*, and our job is to figure out the *how*." Of course, he was talking about many of the combat missions he had completed where the objective and the measure of success were straightforward. But the executive sat there slack-jawed for a moment before saying, "Wow. That's so simple. That's not only what I need to do with my team; it's how I need to coach my CEO to work with me and my peers."

Think about your intent as a leader. Are you creating a rhythm where there is absolute clarity so it's easy for others to follow you? Keep in mind when we have the freedom to decide the *how*, we're shown that we are trusted, and that expectation stimulates us to be intrinsically motivated to be adaptive, creative, and resourceful. Clarity is the precursor for the collective commitment that creates a team rhythm and makes work fulfilling and fun!

▲▲▲

Now take a moment to consider your own organization and how you approach helping your team members develop rhythm:

- Does everyone clearly understand their roles and responsibilities so they are on the same page?
- Is the pace steady, predictable, and reliable but with an ability to change quickly and easily without losing momentum or people getting frustrated?
- Do people enjoy each other's company, and is there cohesion versus cliques?

## THE REST OF THE STORY

It is always hard to lead on the last day, and Sal made a lot of assumptions about his role and how the group dynamic had evolved. We wish we could report that Sal recognized the synergy of his team and adapted his approach and plan to maintain the rhythm, but he did not. Throughout the entire trip, Sal was quiet and struggling, because he was ill-prepared for the journey. He suffered in silence, but his suffering was known to all. And the group helped, encouraged, and worked hard not to let him get down on himself. Yet, on that last day, Sal's energy and enthusiasm were off the chart as if he had something to prove in his ability to lead. Despite having seasoned leaders, and a return route that was the same as the one they had ascended into the mountains, Sal attempted to gain and maintain control, leading the team as if they were rookies and the route was unknown.

His leadership style was a complete mismatch, and all the support he'd gained over the expedition evaporated as he repeatedly tried to exert control, which interfered with the team's rhythm. It was obvious as they were within a couple miles of the parking lot that the team had become less a fine-tuned orchestra and more like an improv jazz session with mediocre musicians all playing the kazoo!

But then something remarkable happened. After the trek that showed moments of real team rhythm, the team wanted to give him honest feedback, but also protect his pride. They demonstrated care and compassion, and honored him with their truth. He had missed the mark badly by failing to recognize the team's demonstrated strengths and capabilities, and he disrupted the rhythm. With knowledge of what he was wrestling with at work and on the home front, however, they provided compassionate feedback he could use to improve life back at home. They also asked open-ended questions (not leading, accusatory questions) to help him self-discover and improve his self-awareness so he could see the path forward to grow into the leader he wants to be—the leader his future teams need him to be. The team's rhythm was regained not because it was leader-led, but because it was team-led. The team had developed a strong baseline of trust coupled with a common purpose that resulted in a rhythm that could still withstand a disrupted cadence while overcoming adversity.

## CONCLUSION

We are often asked what the most important thing is that we need to do to preserve culture. Our short answer is, "Uphold the values of the organization." Our longer answer is that culture is about creating an environment where purpose is clear and shared accountability is seen as a sacred duty to not let other people down, especially when it comes to commitments, promises, and obligations. When a team fires on all cylinders, they create synergy and achieve an unmistakable rhythm they can feel deep down in their bones.

Alignment comes from a leader's focus on creating a team rhythm built upon a common purpose directed toward a common goal. Creating and maintaining that rhythm demands a combination of vision, discipline, effectiveness, and adaptability, all with an ingrained sense of duty at the core. The strong, regular, repeated pattern of movement leads to a collective state of flow in which progress for the organization becomes inevitable. Communication is seamless. The team acts as one. Without that palpable rhythm, individual commitment and team performance are at risk. However, an environment that enhances team members' ability to identify and respond to each other's needs allows them to work together in ways that were previously unimaginable.

## THE THREE PILLARS

### *Leading Self*

Rhythm begins with the leader. If you lack clarity on where you are going, why, and how to get there, there is no way you can effectively communicate to your team and build a selfless commitment among the team along the way.

- How do you describe the vision, mission, and values of your organization so they resonate with individual drivers?
- In what ways can you inspire selflessness toward the mission?
- What stories can you use to make expectations come alive to gain commitment and ownership?

### *Leading Others*

In order to create a true rhythm, you have to ensure that each teammate is capable of holding their own while coming together in service of the larger organization. The whole fails if even one person isn't meeting expectations.

- How can you foster a sense of collective discipline without it feeling oppressive and micromanaged?
- What behaviors should be observed that indicate respect and trust exist at all levels?
- What can you do proactively to ensure that issues are handled expediently and effectively when they arise on the team?

### *Leading the Organization*

Leadership requires a light touch. Any hint of micromanagement and you can create an "us" vs. "them" environment, in which employees feel like they constantly have to be on the defense. Such an attitude makes it nearly impossible to create a sustainable, dynamic rhythm. Remember, *people support what they help create.* By giving employees the responsibility to discover problems, and develop solutions, they'll be more committed to the organization's success.

- How can you create an adaptable environment that is also efficient?
- What is your average engagement score as an organization? What one improvement would make the biggest difference and increase your score?
- How can you ingrain a shared sense of duty that becomes a steadfast value? Who can help you clarify and communicate the expected process?

CHAPTER 10

# TRIBAL CONNECTIONS

## *Cementing Commitments*

> "Downhill was way easier—even joyful. Unlike at the beginning, we were talking about how to take our work forward, and all the possibilities. We were encouraging each other about self and peer discovery and how we were going to use what we learned."
>
> —*Sheryl Tullis, Executive and Veteran Participant, Wallowa Mountains in Eastern Oregon*

At the end of every Crucible, participants are asked to perform an appreciation exercise, similar to the one described in chapter five, which takes place on the last night of the trek. Huddled around the campfire, there is a swirling mix of emotions—disappointment the experience is coming to a close, excitement to reach their final goal, a sense of gratitude for the friendships made, and general feelings of satisfaction that come from accomplishing something difficult. During the exercise, participants tell each team member what they appreciate about him or her. The focus stays on one person at a time.

Team members take a turn describing the positive attributes they've seen in each other, and often, what they see as a person's potential to make an even bigger impact on the lives of others.

It is often an emotional experience. Many of the leaders are senior level, and the higher they are in the hierarchy of an organization, the less they routinely receive unfiltered and honest feedback, even if it's positive. Often, the positive feedback executives do receive at work comes from subordinates who can be ingratiating, so those compliments lose their impact. However, on the Crucible, people aren't positioning for future gain. Everyone knows the feedback they receive is unvarnished, and it can be eye-opening, even life-changing.

One senior executive who participated in the Moab Crucible described the experience as one of the strongest of the whole expedition. When her turn came to share her appreciation, she took the time to personalize her thoughts about each person on the team. She was surprised by the responses, as a number of executives and veterans began to cry, because they were so strongly moved by her delivery. As she later explained, many of those leaders rarely receive the type of love and respect she conveyed in her candid compliments. "It was very touching," she said. "It was lovely. Everyone said something positive about others. It was intended to be an affirmation; and it reminded me that affirmation is an incredibly powerful tool—because affiliation must precede affirmation."

Imagine sitting around the campfire, one last time, with a dozen people you've known for only a few days. Now you're in the spotlight, the absolute center of attention. Each member of the expedition is sharing something they appreciate about you in how you showed up, made others think, made others feel, and how you served the team for the greater good. The compliments and insights teammates share aren't surface level. It's always hard for participants to imagine doing a similar exercise with people back at the office, unless they, too, went through something difficult together.

The exercise helps people learn insights about your previously unknown blind spots. Things others know about you that you don't recognize about yourself are illuminated. You begin to understand how much people appreciate even your quirks. You also develop new interpretations of your effect on others. Some points of self-awareness are validated as you get feedback that affirms that which you already knew about yourself. Meanwhile, you have the opportunity to provide the same gift to your teammates, to give more than you receive. By providing your unique insights to others, you help them become more effective, leverage their strengths, and learn more about how they're perceived.

This exercise takes two to three hours, but the time flies by. Everyone is engaged and committed, and the resulting insights are often profound. For many, the exercise can provide an emotional breakthrough, as the words from new friends come from the heart, and the accuracy of the comments validates many participants' own long-lost self-awareness and confidence. The exercise can also be a catalyst for sharpening the saw, thinking bigger, and being truly aspirational in each person's pursuits as they refine their own heroic journey. It's the moment when participants move from "I can" or "I should" to "I will."

On the last morning of the expedition, as described in the previous chapter, the team takes fewer breaks, and they talk with each other more as they travel out of the wilderness. There's always a celebratory feel in the air. Although it might be the same route in reverse from just a few days before, the experience is different on the way back, because *they* are different on the way back. They have forged new relationships and a new understanding of each other and themselves. As one participant said, "Final conversations were much more future focused and we discussed how we were going to really stay connected."

In that final leg of the trek, the team realizes how provisional experiences can be, and that the Crucible will end. Conversations shift to what happens next, and how they'd like their newfound friends to hold them accountable for the commitments they've made to themselves, each other, at work, and even to their family. Sometimes these commitments are new habits that teammates want to change, such as journaling or exercising, realizing that when they actually commit to taking care of themselves they are able to be more self-reliant. Other times the commitments focus on what they want to create for their teams and organizations, such as finally tackling wicked company problems like inefficient processes or a stagnant sales pipeline.

The connection with others allows you to commit, to take ownership for your own development and other responsibilities, and ask the "tribe" to assist you in being accountable for your duty to self, others, and the organization. Tribal commitments are promises that stem from real friendships, where people can call on each other whenever there is an urgent need. The Crucible provides the potential to develop real friends, and as discussed in chapter four, the research is clear that if you have work friends you like, trust, and respect, your engagement and happiness is lifted substantially.[1] In the following section, we share the how-to for leading and leveraging the social capital that exists between people—for people.

## ACCEPTING OWNERSHIP

Leaders often say something along the following lines when describing their ideal team members: "I want my people to take pride and ownership in their work. I don't want to be a micromanager—I want to delegate so I can be more strategic." Let's start right there. What can *you* do, regardless of your position, to accept more ownership and personal responsibility for what others are counting on you to do?

The tribal commitments from the Crucible hold each individual responsible for their own success, as well as for accepting responsibility for their accountability partner. If you fail to uphold your commitment, you must own that, but so, too, does your partner, who should have been checking in on you to ensure you were following through, nudging you when you stumbled. It's likely that we all stumble in creating new habits, but when we assume ownership of all our obligations, and we know our partner also assumes ownership toward the goal, an environment is created that cements the chance for positive outcomes.

### *Know What You Control*

When it comes to accepting ownership, you must first acknowledge what you actually control. What's in your control can typically be boiled down to how you spend your time and how you respond to people and the circumstances before you. If your partner doesn't stick to his or her commitment, that is not ultimately on you; you cannot control your partner's follow-through. What you can control is the commitment you made to check in and provide support and encouragement; if you fail to do that, you own some of the responsibility for your partner not keeping his or her commitment.

With regard to your precious time, you must exercise the self-discipline to say "no" to new commitments that take you away from your imperatives. Saying "no" requires you to be deliberate about your real priorities—what will provide the greatest value toward the objective. It takes self-control to sacrifice things you might enjoy or would rather do, but doing so with the knowledge that the long-term gain is worthwhile makes it easier. Keep in mind, big accomplishments are always incremental—they are never immediate, and they often take weeks, months, or years. But if you prioritize such accomplishments, the achievement of these aspirations is well worth it. As described in chapter four, to uncover your true priorities, ask yourself, "For how long will this matter?"

The other side of the coin is how you respond to people and the circumstances before you. Whereas time management requires discipline, your responses should be based on your ability to harness restraint in order to be thoughtful, measured, and appropriate. When interacting with people, our aim is to influence them in a positive and energizing way. This doesn't mean being right all the time; this means employing acute and active listening and processing what you hear. The more you learn about the situation, the better your response and ability to influence most effectively. It's a process of listening to others, learning by assessing the answers you get from your questions, and then leading with intentionality.

### *Commitments Are a Promise*

Throughout your life, people have invested in you. They have asked questions, listened, offered counsel, and provided advice. Maybe they've been a set of ears to vent to, or a shoulder to cry on. Regardless, they have taken the time to develop a relationship with you, and they likely expect some form of reciprocity, usually just appreciation or a sincere thank-you. In return, you need to provide the same care, attention, and devotion you have received. That can come in the form of taking the advice offered, and actually following up to provide feedback on the helpfulness of counsel. Either way, when ideas are shared, and advice and suggestions are offered, a commitment is created. In many cases, friends want each other to hold them accountable for doing what they said they would do. The best way to ensure expectations remain aligned is to consider a commitment a promise. Jan's co-host on *The Leadership Podcast*, Jim Vaselopulos, has observed that people let obligations fall through the cracks all the time, but no one feels good about breaking a promise.

To be trustworthy and predictable, you have to be reliable. There are commitments you know you have failed to keep, but don't ignore these. Gain an understanding of whether the commitment was realistic at the time you made it and what the obstacle was that prevented you from keeping it, whether internal or external. There may also be commitments you don't even realize you made or missed, and for those you need to find out why. Asking those closest to you about your reliability, and for specific examples where you weren't dependable, can be invaluable in increasing your understanding about what gets in the way of keeping your promises.

### *It's Okay to Ask for Help*

Part of taking ownership is knowing you can't do it all, all by yourself. Every successful person we know has instrumental supporters. Those supporters are mentors, coaches, bosses, parents, clergy, friends, colleagues, and coworkers. Counsel from others helps you assume ownership and personal responsibility for the commitment you make. Confidence and vulnerability go hand in hand, and it's important to remember we're all a work in progress. Being humble enough to open yourself up and seek support will help you develop the genuine confidence required to set and achieve bold goals and heroic aspirations.

Ask for help. Ask for assistance. Ask for input, advice, suggestions, feedback, and accountability. Most importantly, ask yourself the hard questions about what you want, why you want it, what you're willing to do to get it, and what you're willing to give up. Further, recognize that the achievement alone isn't a destination that will make you happy and fulfilled. As Simon Sinek reminds us, "It's the journey, it's the journey, it's the journey."[2] There is no "there."

## APPRECIATION

Fostering a sense of belonging boils down to a few simple tenets: appreciation, lack of repercussions for vulnerability, and catching people doing the right things. Quarterly or annual recognition programs can add value to the culture of your organization, but they are not enough. People have to understand every day that their engagement and commitment to the organization is truly appreciated. Think about the impact of the appreciation exercise described in the chapter opening—authentic and heartfelt appreciation for the way teammates showed up and the impact they had on others. When you take the time to genuinely recognize people, you are not just "thanking them for doing their job," but you are amplifying their engagement, resilience, and sense of belonging.

If we are embracing a growth mindset, as Carol Dweck would advise, we will all stumble and need support from others, no matter how self-reliant we are. When we are striving to build a culture in which people are working to improve, we must ensure that there aren't negative repercussions when teammates don't understand, ask for help, or make mistakes. When we make it unsafe for people to be vulnerable, we build a culture in which everyone stays in their comfort zone with no significant competitive advantage.

In fact, we'd suggest you go a step further than just ensuring there are no repercussions for vulnerability—amplify the behaviors you are looking for. Doing so will accelerate the true sense of belonging and commitment to the team. Because the business world operates at such a high speed, please, thank you, and a general appreciation for others often get overlooked. It's important to help people at all levels know they matter, their job matters, and they truly belong as vital members of the team. It's through communicating real appreciation that the foundation of trust is solidified, and dedication and a sense of duty, and perhaps even loyalty, to one another flourishes.

Appreciation and recognition are the greatest ways leaders can nourish the intrinsic motivators that lie within us all. Doing difficult things together, whether scaling a glacier, preparing for a major board meeting, or guiding teammates through tough times, can forge an indomitable team. Overcoming the difficulties together is what creates a real sense of belonging during the Crucible experience.

## *Motivation Matters*

When we appreciate people, we can best influence them to cement their commitments. But motivation also plays a role. Scholars in business and psychology have studied motivation for more than fifty years, including how we motivate ourselves (intrinsic motivation) and how we can motivate others (extrinsic motivation). No matter how amazing the incentives we apply to motivate others, the research is consistent: intrinsic motivation will take us farther and last longer. When we truly want to motivate and engage our teammates, we have to help them discover their credibility, agency, relationships, and purpose.

It is hard to maintain your determination and persistence if you do not feel *credible* in your work. If you do not have the competence to be trusted to do what you are being asked, you will likely find a reason to shift your energy elsewhere. When a teammate knows they have the credibility needed to achieve the outcome, leaders must get out of the way and let them own *how* the task will be completed. Nothing is more demoralizing for teammates than to have their *agency* taken from them by a leader who micromanages them or tells them how to accomplish the task. Empowerment is motivating.

Healthy cultures allow teammates to ask for help when needed and to hold each other accountable to promises made. We need belonging, which requires a safe environment. Knowing that our strong *relationships* are there for when we need them, we have the capacity to keep pushing through hard times.

Finally, without a solid sense of *purpose*, it will be nearly impossible to sustain a high level of motivation, even with credibility, agency, and strong relationships. Do you have absolute clarity when it comes to your purpose and aspirations? How about those of your team? If the connection with the purpose is unclear, leaders need to help their teammates connect personal purpose to the organizational purpose, or a mundane task to the larger goal.

When leaders take the time to understand each teammate as an individual, recognizing the unique skills they bring to the team (credibility), *how* they best work toward goal completion (agency), in which ways they most appreciate team support (relationships), and deliberately connect the work with personal and organizational meaning (purpose), they will find they have teams who are motivated to go farther and faster than they previously thought possible. These teammates will achieve their commitments because they have pride in themselves, and a respect for a team they would not dream of letting down.

### Cultivate Obligations

The leader has the ultimate responsibility to create an expectation that each team member also has an obligation to assume personal responsibility to produce results and exercise empathy to foster an environment of belonging. When it comes to obligations, it is important for leaders to ensure each person understands that not every organization is a giant, well-funded tech company with highly educated, white-collar labor. Most organizations have a diverse work population, limited resources, stakeholders to satisfy, and obligations to meet, like payroll or service levels. Few firms are corporate behemoths, and most are entities created by an entrepreneur who at one time took an enormous risk to start and build a business.

These job creators put it all on the line to fulfill their vision to meet a market need and scaled to the point where they realized they couldn't fulfill their obligations without the help of others. That's how jobs get created, dreams get fulfilled, families are provided for, and ultimately, people have the opportunity to find purpose and meaning in the service of others. It's ultimately the leader's responsibility to ensure that people work together where the environment is one where we "get" to do our work versus a dreaded obligatory "have" to. That opportunity—and obligation—will breed commitment to one another and the goal at hand.

### *Team One vs. Team Two*

At work, most every leader has more than one team to which they belong. The members of team one may come as a surprise—they are not the people you lead. Team one consists of your leader and your peers. Team two is made up of your immediate direct reports. Stanford professor of organizational behavior Jeffrey Pfeffer often challenges conventional assumptions about leadership. A major point he makes is that "the first responsibility of a leader is to keep their job. The second is to get things done."[3] There's a strong correlation between leaders who lose their job and a poor relationship with upper management and peers, or team one. It may be because leaders are too focused on team two.

We can empathize with a leader who focuses all of their team-building effort on the team they lead with the sincere belief that their role as a leader is in service to their direct reports. Ultimately, however, as Pfeffer illustrates, if leaders fail to create a community and a culture of belonging among team one, they are less able to serve team two. That's because they will lack the power and influence within the organization that is derived from the reciprocal relationships in team one.

In the context of the different levels of teams, Pfeffer infers that if you don't invest in the relationships with your peers, leaders, and partners, you aren't going to be effective at getting resources and removing obstacles for direct reports. Further, if you are unable to get things done, someone else is going to step in and create influence in ways that could profoundly impact both your effectiveness and your fate—often at the peril of your current role.

If you are paid to lead, you need to have teammates in team two who are inspired to follow you, but you can't lose sight of the team one constituents with whom you must also build trust and influence. Keep a broad perspective, and don't become so focused on one team that you neglect the other. Deliver on your commitments to all parties, and when your tribal connections are strong with everyone, you will be able to secure commitments from others, no matter what team they are on.

## CREATE THE ENVIRONMENT

It is possible to have a team of gritty leaders who are highly motivated to achieve the goals of the organization, but who flounder or fail to uphold their commitments because of the culture. Organizational behavior is not only a result of the personalities of the people on the team, but of the environment in which they operate.

By creating a safe environment, you develop better connections and foster positive attitudes that stay strong despite adversity. These may include an expectation that there will be significant difficulties, and people must have the willingness to face them; a comfort in using humor, in which the job and purpose are taken seriously, though allowing room for appropriate jokes and self-deprecation; an understanding that you need to risk saying what you think with genuine vulnerability; and last, a fearlessness to think big. When multiple people on a team have the same positive attitudes, an environment is created where resilience is collectively strengthened. People, like iron, are forged through fire. That's the environment in which crucibles are conquered.

### *Autonomy and Interdependence*

A survey from 2022 indicated that 40 percent of people were thinking about quitting their job. There were a number of findings that spoke to the reasons why, including leaders being out of touch with their employees, and high productivity masking an exhausted workforce. Meanwhile, the survey found that cultural trends were affecting the workplace. Shrinking networks were endangering innovation, and Generation Z workers needed to be reenergized in order to be retained.[4] Dynamic and hybrid work arrangements are here to stay, and leaders must figure out how to provide motivating autonomy along with fostering the interdependence that yields exceptional breakthroughs.

If you are struggling with how to lead such work arrangements where people remain engaged and collaborative, even when not co-located, consider asking yourself (and your team) the following five questions:

1. Do you have a bias that people who want flexibility are less loyal, less committed, and less engaged? What does the evidence you've collected show?
2. If you have a part of the workforce who must be physically present (e.g., services and manufacturing), do you think it's unfair that office workers in the same organization have a choice about where they work? Why?
3. Are you sure you're not operating with outdated control issues, or find that you simply don't trust your team?
4. Have you thought about how your current policies may affect your future goals to be more inclusive and diverse?
5. Are there other options you haven't considered with regard to where people work, when they work, and how they collaborate?

The point is that work has forever changed, and now comes with different complexities for today's leader. Without robust networks, strong connections will be elusive. And without those strong connections, the sense of belonging that comes with being part of an indomitable team is lost. No belonging, no commitments.

### *Adapt and Adjust*

A baseball announcer once told us the story of a sixty-eight-year-old first-base coach, a man who knew everything about coaching first base. He could read a pitcher's intent and tell if he was going to throw to the first baseman to keep the runner from stealing second. He recognized a pitcher's confidence and fear, and he understood how to calm the nerves of the runner on first base. His expertise relative to the game was the same over the years, but his approach to the players adapted to the times. He coached twenty-four-year-old professional baseball players in 2023 differently than he did in 2016. And he coached twenty-four-year-old professional baseball players in 2011 differently than he coached those in 2016. The coach didn't lower the standards, though he adjusted his coaching to best influence and gain commitment from the players of the moment.

That's what we have to do to cement our commitments with one another: adapt and adjust. Everything continues to change. It doesn't mean lower your standards, but alter your approach to reach the person you're working with today. If you're not able to accommodate all the demands of today's workforce, just make sure you're up front about where you can, where you can't (or won't), and why.

Be intentional about collaboration. Make work a place to meet, greet, and innovate. Don't waste the time that you have with your team through death by PowerPoint, status updates, or demotivating rants about missed goals. People should be excited to come to your meetings because they are interactive opportunities to collaborate with colleagues they trust and respect. If your meetings could have been shared in an email, you are missing a key opportunity to enhance relationships, build culture, and cement commitments.

**PRO TIP**

The tribal nature of human connections cannot be overstated. We seek out people who have the same values we do, who believe what we believe, and have similar interests, experiences, and aspirations. In hiring, this is often referred to as "culture fit." While it's natural to seek out connections with like-minded individuals, it's also important to recognize the power of diversity in promoting effective debate, decision-making, and unfettered action. Remain mindful that inadvertent, invisible barriers limit participation and prevent individuals from feeling like they belong, even when others on the team or in the organization have the best of intentions. Prioritize inclusivity and encourage diverse perspectives to get everyone fully engaged and actively participating. Instead of "culture fit," look for people who will be a "culture add" and will bring value to your team through different and unique perspectives.

▲▲▲

Now take a moment to consider your own organization and how you approach cementing commitments among your team members:

- How can you better foster and nurture deep and meaningful connections among team members—especially with people who are seldom in the same place at the same time?
- How would you describe the benefit of an environment where team members openly share their aspirations for, and fears around, personal growth and collective learning?
- In what ways can you promote the principle of reciprocity within teams to ensure bonds among team members are built on trust and shared accountability?

## THE REST OF THE STORY

When one team member got back home from the Crucible, he broke down into tears while telling his wife about the experience. As he explained, "I don't know exactly why, it was just a powerful experience. I learned so much and got to know people so deeply in just four days. The challenge gave me a unique opportunity to learn about what I really want my life to be about as someone who wants to lead others more effectively." Another participant observed, "If I needed to, I could call anyone from that trip today for anything."

Many Crucible participants have a moving experience, and they start to see the world—and their duty in it—through a different lens after they complete an expedition. Their drive for success and willingness to overcome obstacles changes significantly—and persists. Within a year of completing one Patagonia Crucible, most of the participants made a significant change to focus on pursuing work with purpose and meaning, and they made commitments to hold each other accountable for their goals and aspirations.

## CONCLUSION

The Crucible offers a truly exceptional and rare opportunity to forge fast and profound friendships, distinguished by remarkably strong bonds. It's those bonds—those deep and meaningful human connections—where dreams are shared, aspirations expanded, and commitments formed. These bonds follow the rule of reciprocity, as in any functional relationship. Former Coast Guard officer Meghan Zehringer summed up how the connections she made led to validation, and later, award-winning success as an executive: "What I learned from [the Crucible] changed my personal and professional life for good, and it completely blew all my other leadership training out of the water. In my military career I was given commendations, was lauded on all of my evaluations, and I was praised by senior Coast Guard leadership. None of this gave me the sense of validation that I got from [the Crucible]."[5] It's the same even if you're not on an expedition in the wilderness. Tribal connections help people feel safe enough to ask for help, assume ownership for their own actions, and ultimately cement commitments to and for each other.

## THE THREE PILLARS

### *Leading Self*

Owning your strengths and weaknesses is a commitment to lifelong learning.

- What is one strength that served you well in the past, but can now sometimes be a derailer?
- Who can provide unvarnished feedback on your reliability and reputation?
- What holds you back from asking for help? How does that affect your growth, and your effectiveness with others?

### *Leading Others*

Catching people doing things right requires leaders to hear the unheard and see the unseen to cultivate the strengths in others.

- How can you better show appreciation to others, and help the team create a sense of belonging?
- What can you do to improve the current ratio of positive to constructive feedback for all those you work with?
- How can you best guide people to find purpose and meaning in their work?

### *Leading the Organization*

The culture you build doesn't happen by default; it happens by design.

- Are you deliberate about providing the *what* and *why*, and leaving the *how* for others to determine?
- What steps can you take to adapt and adjust your meetings so they're interactive, collaborative, and inspirational?
- What changes could you make to increase your teammates' recruitment of their friends?

CHAPTER 11

# THE CRUX

## *Bringing It All Together*

"We were at our best when we slowed down, war roomed the situation, and pulled out ideas from the entire team. It's amazing how quickly you find consensus when you really get people contributing their thoughts."
—*Jeff Engelstad, Executive Participant, Ouray, Colorado*

Corey was used to being in control. His ability to effectively plan for every contingency was one of the things that had made him so successful in his career. He thought he knew what he was in for on the Crucible, so ahead of the trek he visited his local outdoor adventure store multiple times, ensuring he had all the right gear. In his preparation, he took long walks with a weighted pack around his neighborhood and the unusual step of a hydration IV before departing for the Rocky Mountains' high altitude. He'd done his share of physical activity when he was younger, playing hockey and other team sports, so he felt completely prepared for what was ahead.

As is always the case, we can never truly plan for every contingency. When Corey started the Crucible, he quickly recognized he had not considered the impact of climbing a relentless steep slope compared to a casual walk on even ground. In addition, the extra weight he'd put on in the past few years was affecting his physical performance more than he had expected. It was a harsh realization early in the trip. He felt a mild headache, nausea, and a general fatigue he could have never imagined, all signs pointing to mild altitude sickness. The impact was the result of 14 percent oxygen in the mountains versus the 21 percent at sea level his body was accustomed to. Still, he didn't want to let the team down, so he did his best to mask the effects, turning his grimace into a smile when anyone looked at him, despite how awful he felt.

By the second day, Corey just couldn't hide the struggle any longer. As he slowed the entire team down, he got stuck inside his head. He became extra hard on himself, the fear of disappointing others gnawing at him. At one point, he sat down on the side of a steep climb, not knowing whether he just needed a minute, or if he needed to tell everyone he would have to quit, then work with the team to sort out the logistics of turning around. This was not the experience he had planned for; he was clearly not in control of his body or even his emotions at that moment. It was as if he had two mini versions of himself sitting on each of his shoulders whispering in his ears. The positive version was saying, "Suck it up!" The other, cynical, version asked, "Is this really where you want to be—is this really worth it?"

What happens when we're pushed to our limit? What happens when we accomplish something remarkable, something we once thought was out of reach? What about when we call it quits? During the Crucible, many of the participants find they actually have two experiences. One is during the Crucible when they are in the moment—and oftentimes in their own head, suffering in silence. The other experience is what often happens *after* the Crucible, when they have time to reflect on what it all meant. It's what was said about them in the appreciation exercise during the final fireside chat. It's what they learned from the solo challenge sitting alone in their thoughts for hours with only the distraction of bugs, wind, and weather. It is what they learned by helping others. And it's what they learned about being vulnerable when they allowed someone to help them. Ultimately, all the lessons come down to what they value—what's truly important in how they serve others in their quest for purpose and meaning in their life.

How we ask ourselves hard questions, and when we choose to answer them honestly, portends how we will react in tough situations; it also shows who we are as leaders. On a Crucible, the crux is the moment participants recognize they want to quit, but don't. It's a feeling of crossing the chasm and accepting the suffering, because you realize that's part of becoming stronger, more resilient, and relentlessly tenacious. It's the moment in which everything you've experienced throughout an expedition comes together in a quiet acknowledgment that you did indeed succeed.

The crux may be different for each individual, even on the same expedition. As one Crucible participant commented, her crux occurred when she found herself taking a risk even when she wasn't in control of the situation. During the early part of the expedition in the Rocky Mountains, she felt out of her element, uncertain of herself and uncomfortable with the many unknowns—the people, the terrain, her backpack, everything. She was the slowest person in the group, barely able to keep up. This was especially hard for her because she had never been the person others had to wait on. She also had to rely on others at almost every turn, needing help to cross creeks, get up the rocky, uneven terrain, and even put her backpack on.

What surprised her was that people wanted to assist her because it gave them purpose. Supporting her made them feel good. She realized that setting her own pride and ego aside helped others build the team.

And over those days together, she learned to face her fear as every leader does, asking, "What am I so afraid of?" This was a transformative experience that provided a new perspective about what others may feel when they're the weak link. In the end, being vulnerable made her mentally stronger to work through the suffering and the struggle, and ultimately enabled her to rally. In fact, this person demonstrated an astonishing handstand on a mountaintop at 13,000 feet to the cheers of the entire team!

The crux comes down to what's really important, because if it is, people will pay the price—be it sacrifice, discipline, or even suffering. When decisions and actions are guided by values, this foundation holds firm and will not crumble. It allows the leader to lead oneself and others, and effectively guide the organization.

## WHEN THE TRAITS ALIGN

It takes discipline to assume personal responsibility to learn, sharpen, and hone knowledge into skills, all while developing character traits that enable you to lead effectively and remain reliable to others. Sacrifice is also needed, because you have to place others' needs before your own. This means putting in more hours, preparing in more detail, being there for people during inconvenient times, and knowing it will be harder for you than anyone on your team to role model the ideal balance of work and home; of fitness and endurance; of preparation and delivery; and of stoicism and authenticity. The crux is when these traits all align, you get the aha, and it all comes together.

Successful and fulfilled people use their discipline to set boundaries and balance their priorities with regard to how they spend their time on what they consider most important. These may include one of the five Fs: family, faith, finances, fitness, and fulfillment. By the end of our journey in the woods, across deserts, or in canyons, the teams on the

Crucibles find a new orientation toward fulfillment, recognizing that when we lead ourselves first and find our personal success in family, faith, finances, and fitness, we have a strong base in order to pursue fulfillment focused on others. This type of fulfillment is much deeper and more lasting than mere happiness. Quite simply, self-reliance is not the prerequisite for pleasure-seeking activities that make you happy, but for personal, genuine fulfillment that can only come from the sacrifices required to serve others.

This type of fulfillment can be thought of as "good tired," the kind when you collapse into bed at night knowing that, regardless of the outcome, you gave everything you had to something that deeply mattered to you that day; the kind of tired when you have nothing left to give but the smile on your face. The late, great singer-songwriter Harry Chapin described good tired in an interview as such: "It's that good tired, ironically enough, can be a day that you lost, but you don't even have to tell yourself because you knew you fought your battles, you chased your dreams, you lived your days and when you hit the hay at night, you settle easy, you sleep the sleep of the just."[1]

When meeting with clients, we always start by asking how they are doing. In addition to genuinely connecting with them, we're looking for something we can celebrate to start off on a positive note. But the first response is almost always an exasperated, "Crazy busy—a lot going on!" Our coaching starts with acknowledging that "addicted to busy" mindset. Through our subsequent questions and discussions, we get people to slow down and reflect, helping them realize that the investment they're making in their self-awareness to adapt to a complex, busy world is one important mark of a self-reliant leader. But this self-awareness is just a starting point; there are other attributes for a self-reliant leader to develop and pull together before they can truly get to that crux. They don't come easy, and their emergence is often hard won. But once you recognize them, you can then practice them, day in and day out. Though we've hit on some of these attributes earlier in the book, let's take a closer look to see how they can all come together, starting with knowing thyself.

## *Know Thyself*

A deep understanding of your strengths, weaknesses, and what you stand for in terms of your moral and ethical values leads to true self-awareness. You must also recognize how your words and deeds affect others. Further, you need the discipline to self-regulate and deliver a response that serves the needs of the team, not what satisfies your own pride or ego. You must placate your insecurities and still lead authentically. To really look within, ask yourself about your own purpose, values, and goals:

- **Purpose.** For whose good do you serve? When you look around at how your skills and interests can be used to serve others, what do you see? Who are the people you most want to help, and by doing what? Some people have a job, others have a career, and the lucky few have a calling, doing what they love because it provides them with deep purpose and meaning. What would it take for you to wake up thinking, *I get to* . . . versus *I have to* . . . ?
- **Values.** What do you hold dear? What are the things you care so deeply about that you'd be willing to fight for them? These questions are about knowing the lines you won't cross, and how you will operate to fulfill your purpose. Many people will cite honesty, integrity, and truth, but consider what exactly causes you to like, trust, and respect others. What do you need to do to have that reciprocated?
- **Goals.** What does success look like for you? For some, it might be material wealth or financial security. For others, it might be a functional family. Still, for others, it might be making a real difference in the world to improve people's lives. One thing is for certain: a good life is defined on your terms, no one else's.

> Start with ensuring that your short- and mid-term goals are truly aligned with your longer-term vision. When you're living a good life, you'll be good tired at the end of every day.

Understanding your purpose, values, and goals allows you to uncover your blind spots, and opens you up to a genuine curiosity of others. This curiosity can also result in a focus on how you come across to people. That focus leads to a process of sharpening the saw to exert greater influence in the right way, at the right time, with the right people, for the right reasons. Seeking feedback, focusing on learning, and honing your purpose gets you closer to true fulfillment.

A concrete way to help know thyself is through journaling. Even in the midst of the wilderness, Crucible participants are invited to spend time alone with their thoughts, a pen, and a small notebook. Some participants find this activity to be the hardest of the expedition; but it's often when people begin to make sense of what they are experiencing. In order to guide this learning process, each person is given a small notebook for their reflections, and the framework in a credit card–like format. To help them gain understanding of themselves in their current environment, and how they want to show up in the next days, they are prompted with these questions on the card:

1. Rate your day. What criteria did you use? Were those criteria made up of things you control?
2. What are you grateful for? Why? Does that align with your top values—that is, what you hold dear?
3. What did you learn? How would you categorize that learning? Are you focused on learning new skills, approaches, and concepts that will get you closer to your goals?
4. What is the single priority for tomorrow? What will be the outcome of that priority? Can you really focus and say no to less important duties others can handle?

When you journal consistently, you're able to discern useful patterns, such as actions that make a great day, your focus with regard to learning and growth, and incremental progress on milestones to achieve your aspirational goals. After a Crucible to the Wallowa Mountains, one of the participants had this to say about the journaling experience: "When journaling, my takeaway was the importance of quiet time and not just being busy all of the time. I now block time for no meetings, take time off for vacations so I can pause and reflect. I get a lot more done now, and better outcomes, too."

Journaling can accelerate your ability to understand your own journey, and build a life that leads to fulfillment. The following questions are helpful in building self-awareness and worth revisiting regularly in your journaling practice:

1. In what ways am I showing up for those most important to me? What else might they need from me?
2. How am I leading in alignment with my values? How am I not?
3. What goals have I set around my finances? Am I taking steps today to meet those goals? What adjustments can I make?
4. How am I taking care of myself physically (including diet, exercise, and sleep)?
5. What will move me closer to fulfillment, providing the greatest impact on those I serve?

Without knowing thyself, you will lack the ability to recognize the impact your actions have on those around you. Slowing down to make sense of your experiences will allow you to grow exponentially.

### *Personal Responsibility*

Personal responsibility requires leaders to be uncomfortable and have the situational humility to say, "I was wrong." "I made a mistake." "I am sorry." "I don't understand." You must be willing to take ownership of your actions and decisions, while also being bold enough to take reasonable risks. Most importantly, you must accept responsibility and remain accountable for everything your team does, or fails to do. As a self-reliant leader, you need to role model a strong work ethic and creative, transparent, problem-solving skills.

As General Stan McChrystal (author of the foreword) explains, there is only one thing all leaders have in common: "It's a willingness to sacrifice for the cause when they decide to lead."[2] When asked to lead, they raised their hand. They volunteered to accept more responsibility. They are willing to lead, which is a risk in itself, and they acknowledge potential failure. Leaders step up, especially when others can't, won't, or don't. They are the ones willing to sacrifice a comfortable, calm, predictable, and stress-free existence. Their commitment to the mission, to the team, to the people, and to all stakeholders is absolute.

## Clear Goals and Objectives

While you need a clear vision of where you want to take your team, it is equally important that you effectively communicate this vision through the use of stories, metaphors, or analogies (note, a metaphor uses imagery to elicit an emotional response or feeling, whereas an analogy uses comparative imagery to help others think and deduce). You must not only take into account the direction your team is headed, but how you want your people to feel about the journey in which they're participating. Remember: *People support what they help create.* When the team understands and supports the vision, they take ownership, and you can spend less time holding teammates accountable.

The vision is a destination, even if it feels unachievable, and it's powered by the team's shared purpose and goals. During a Crucible in Oregon, the participants were told they were going to summit a ten-thousand-foot peak where there were no existing trails. In response, someone raised their hand and asked, "Why are we climbing this mountain?" As you know by now, by design, Crucibles purposely push people from their comfort zones, helping them to develop a new understanding about themselves and the world around them. So it was curious to us that someone asked *why* we were going to climb this peak. Feeling a bit incredulous, we gathered our thoughts as we realized, this person really needs to know *why*. It was obvious to us why we were making this climb, but that didn't matter. It was not obvious to him. And that lack of knowledge was on us.

We took a deep breath, mustered our patience, and explained how the trek would involve teamwork, leadership, communication, and decision-making, and the bonus was that everyone would be rewarded with a sense of accomplishment, astonishing views, and pictures to memorialize the joint effort. To our amazement, he simply nodded and replied, "Okay." And that was that. Once the "why" was made apparent, this teammate was all in; without it, he was skeptical. How many times do we fail to provide our team with the clarity of *why* we are doing a particular task because we assumed they knew? We often see leaders miss the "why" but instead get into the "how." The best leaders let the team figure out the how.

### *Strong Decision-Making Skills*

The late General Colin Powell famously said that when you face a tough decision, you should have at least 40 percent and no more than 70 percent of the information required to make it. If you have less than 40 percent, you don't have enough information, and if you have more than 70 percent, you have probably waited too long for the decision to create a competitive advantage. One thing is for certain: unlike many of the veterans who have participated in Crucibles, and had to make instantaneous life and death decisions in combat, most of us are fortunate that very few business decisions require split-second decisions.

Your decisions should be intentional, deliberate, thoughtful, and balanced, and you must know when to rely on yourself and when to bring in the group. You will need to make difficult decisions methodically and confidently. If the situation doesn't call for an immediate decision, include others to gather multiple points of view and to ensure you're not missing a critical factor in making the best decision. Dissent is healthy, but when the decision is made, the team must present a unified front. The best decisions are based on criteria according to what the organization truly values; and being focused means saying no more than saying yes.

### *Continuous Curiosity*

Curiosity allows you to look for opportunities to learn and develop, and stay open to coaching and constructive feedback. When veterans and executives are paired together during Crucible Expeditions, the executives are often amazed to hear what these relatively young leaders had to endure in combat. Their war stories don't align with the worldview most of us get from the news. And their tales often remind participants of the sacrifices made, courage exemplified, and how many conveniences we take for granted. At a certain point, we find ourselves reminding the veterans that none of the executives are going to become commandos. And we remind the executives that they aren't here to just hear about leadership through the lens of military application. We ask them both to be more curious about the world in which the veterans are entering and the unique perspective each can bring.

Many of these veterans have become masters at the "problem set." That is, they see a familiar problem and they move decisively, in the fashion they were trained. While many executives would be well served by being more decisive at times, the issue with that decisive approach in business is that you might miss out on asking critical questions that allow you to better understand the problem's root cause, background, and history, along with the ability to identify the people who have dealt with the problem for years or decades. Curiosity is the mark of great leadership, the sign of an effective and compassionate colleague, and is evident in the Socratic approach of the best teachers. As German mathematician Georg Cantor said, "The art of proposing a question must be held of higher value than solving it." Curiosity is the indicator of wisdom.

### *Lead by Example*

When people think of leadership, they most often equate it to leading direct reports, and the day-to-day interaction with a team. But when done well, leading a team helps its members lead each other. Role model the behaviors you wish to see in others. For example, display a healthy relationship between work and personal life. This doesn't mean you should place a wall between the two, but allow for healthy overlap while also setting boundaries that make sense for you. Service to others and service to family, friends, and your own well-being can be intertwined. This balance is critical to remain authentic, so develop a leadership style that works for you, and will inspire others.

Dealing with people who disappoint you, frustrate you, and don't meet your expectations is the best vantage point for you to view yourself. What sort of person are you? Are you kind, patient, understanding? What can you do to get others to do more than they thought they could? Perhaps you can bring out the best in a person, and they can rally, causing the team to get behind them. And remember, when you're the leader, everyone is looking at you to see how you will deal with stressful and difficult situations. Either way, kindness will carry the day, even when you have to be compassionately candid and constructive. As the old saying goes, "Kindness is the language which the deaf can hear and the blind can see."

The leader for the day on a Crucible explained how the team came together in support of a teammate who was struggling on a grueling climb: "The team did a good job of being cool about it and reminded him that we weren't here to break any records, that he can and should pace himself. Someone asked how we could help him get through this and a few people rallied around him to help him pace himself better." The model the leader set for care and consideration of her teammate rippled through the team, and others rose to the occasion. The entire team was better off as a result of compassion instead of criticism or condemnation.

### *An Indomitable Team Spirit*

Regardless of how squared away you are, nobody achieves anything worthwhile alone. The importance of building a team of people that is impossible to subdue or defeat, and who have complementary skills and experience, cannot be overstated. The essence in developing such a team is to exercise judgment by knowing your people, and effectively balance their tasks and deadlines to produce high performance and results.

In Patagonia, the designated leader for the day had been struggling physically, but he never lost his enthusiasm or sense of humor. As soon as he was selected as the leader, he delegated almost every task. "Pete, you work with the guides since you want to be a guide one day. Rich, you set the pace up front, and ensure we're making a beeline to base camp. Bob, make sure the logistics are good—we're getting water when needed, taking the necessary number of breaks, and keeping track of gear. Colin, you were a medic, so I want you watching me and others who are struggling a bit." He delegated the right task to the right person given their natural talents and areas of interest. In the process, he demonstrated trust, allowing his teammates to take ownership of their area of responsibility. He also lightened his leadership load.

Though he delegated almost all of his responsibilities, he did not delegate his *accountability*. If the team had success, it was because of them. If the team made mistakes, or failed, that was on him. During the fireside chat, he led the debrief, and people praised him for his audacity to not even ask for permission to delegate every task. His confidence allowed him to be vulnerable, but more importantly, he trusted the team, and each person rose to the occasion. Trust was reciprocated. No one wanted to let him down, and vice versa. It was a site to behold on how taking a chance, and assuming a risk, elevated his status among the team for the rest of the trip, despite the fact that he was the least capable person in the wilderness.

**PRO TIP**

We've all reached a point where we didn't think we could continue, whether in sports, at work, in school, or in a relationship. Sometimes, we quit, and maybe that was the prudent thing to do at the time. Sometimes, though, we dug deep and achieved more than we thought possible. Oftentimes, when we come through challenges, personally or professionally, we don't slow down to make sense of the experience. Consider taking time now to journal on your own or engage your team in a debrief in order to learn what made the difference in sticking with something or choosing to walk away from it. Did you have grit? Did you make the right call to walk away given the facts, resources, and impact? Make a commitment to yourself that the next time you overcome or sidestep a challenge, you will slow down and gain an understanding of why you took the action you did and what you'd advise yourself to do the next time.

▲▲▲

Now take a moment to consider your own organization and how you approach the crux:

- Under what conditions, and at what point, is there too much hardship for your team?
- What sacrifices in your life will have the longest reaching consequences?
- When it comes to difficulties, what does each *crux* have in common?

## THE REST OF THE STORY

What Corey hadn't counted on when he sat down was a frank conversation with Jacob. Jacob was a tall, lanky, young executive who looked the part of an outdoorsman. He staggered up behind Corey, plopped down next to him, and admitted he was also struggling due to an old ankle injury, but he was trying his best to hide it. As Jacob admitted this truth, he felt the burden of pretending to be stoic start to lift. As they spoke, they both realized that, together, they would muster the stamina to make it to the peak.

John was farther ahead but looked behind him and saw Corey and Jacob sitting side by side—he knew they weren't just taking a break, so he walked back down the mountain to where they were sitting. He chatted with them about effective breathing habits, and as they practiced big breaths, they all started to breathe in unison. When they were ready to get going again, John coached Corey and Jacob on proper footing for steep and rugged slopes, and how to maximize the efficiency of their steps to minimize fatigue. It wasn't long before they were all enjoying lunch at the top.

After lunch, on the way down, Corey began to understand that his own thinking was framing the way he carried himself, and it was not going to improve unless he re-centered himself on aligning his values with his goals. He remembered why he agreed to participate in this expedition in the first place. He wanted to lead more effectively. That's when he accepted the suffering, and realized his crux: compassion and empathy. He thought of his teammates back at the office who were giving their best, but also felt like the "weakest link" at times. He could show much more empathy for his teammates and help illuminate the "why" of the big goals he was asking them to achieve. He could also pay more attention to how people felt, and that might only become apparent by asking more questions. He realized his purpose was serving others, and ensuring they knew he cared.

## CONCLUSION

What happens when you're pushed to your limit? Do you adapt? Do you muster resilience? Do you get gritty? Do you provide optimism, hope, and meaning? Do you energize people to dig deep, sacrifice, endure discomfort, and push through difficulties? Amidst all the challenges we face, we can maintain a fierce optimism when we are grounded in the "why" of our work. It's up to us to find purpose and meaning in our endeavors, and to ensure those we lead also find the purpose and meaning in their work that speaks to them. When we're in an organization that values what we value—with people who value what we value—there's alignment. The crux is when we develop a tenacious sense of duty to those we work with, those we work for, and we're able to demonstrate persistence and determination in the face of audacious challenges. It's our deeds and actions that role model what we wish to see in others.

## THE THREE PILLARS

### *Leading Self*

The best lessons in life come from when we push ourselves beyond what we thought possible and deliberately pause to recognize the lessons we have learned. Our ability to push ourselves further builds up our reservoir of self-reliance, so we're better postured to lead others through challenges.

- Reflecting on your last challenging experience, what did you expect to happen, what actually happened, and what did you learn?
- When you are facing hardship, what allows you to endure?
- What discipline is required to truly serve others?

### *Leading Others*

The team must take responsibility to fully prepare for what lies ahead. A team that trusts each other is capable of conquering great challenges. Viewing uncertainty with the right perspective requires everyone to be "all in," not only for themselves, but for each other.

- How can you help the team lean into each other during times of hardship?
- How can you develop individual and collective emotional intelligence so there is better awareness when some are struggling?
- How can each person on the team build each other's self-reliance in challenging times?

### *Leading the Organization*

Define the problem in more detail than you describe the solution. It's critical to know the team's limitations and what capabilities are required for future capacity. Challenges will come, and while we may not know the shape or timing, we know they're coming, and we must prepare our organizations by developing resilience.

- How can you create greater alignment to support the ability to respond to the unexpected?
- In what ways have you designed and implemented succession planning and development to enhance capabilities of the organization?
- How can you describe the greater purpose in a way that creates realistic optimism across the organization?

CHAPTER 12

# THE END IS ANOTHER BEGINNING

## *Paying It Forward*

> "I knew the Crucible would be a meaningful journey, but I had no idea the power of the connections right away. It reinforced numerous lessons for me, not the least of which was that everyone is on a journey and challenging experiences lead to wisdom. The group was truly exceptional, and it was powerful seeing so many accomplished people still in the process of seeking truth and growth. There are a number of people I plan to stay in touch with to seek advice, and to offer any help I can."
>
> —*Vik Bakshi, Veteran Participant, Ouray, Colorado*

What happens after the Crucible is the metric by which success is ultimately measured. How participants internalize and process their experience matters even more in the subsequent days and weeks as they spread the lessons they've gained in how they treat, mentor, and lead others. When participants return home, they're often inspired to keep the lessons they've learned close at hand. Robert, an executive from a Fortune 500 company who participated in a Crucible in the Wallowa Mountains of Oregon, erased all the tasks on the whiteboard in his office and wrote out the main lessons he'd learned from the Crucible instead. Visible from outside his office, everyone walking by could see what kind of leader he was aspiring to be—including one that was kind, listened well (hearing the unheard), and implicitly trusted his team.

Each week, Robert selected two lessons from the list on which to focus and placed a star next to each. By making his intentions clear, his colleagues, coworkers, and team members were able to provide support, encouragement, and accountability. In a follow-up conversation with him after his Crucible, he spoke about his progress as a leader: "I'm not there yet—I'll never be there, so I have no intention of erasing the lessons from the whiteboard. The Crucible showed me that I needed to break out of the habits I had gotten into as a leader and really change, and my whiteboard was a profound way to create a new habit."

Every journey has an ending, and the hardest part is often making sure the work continues afterward for the intended effect. Recall from chapter nine that when we conclude meetings, we ask, "Who does what by when?" as a way to ensure that commitments and promises are kept, and that the meeting provides a return on time, energy, and dollars. It's the same concept when the Crucible comes to a close. We ask people to pay it forward: What will you do for others, to what effect, and by when?

Paying it forward is the process of instilling a strong sense of purpose, meaning, and commitment in those we're privileged to lead, an essential goodwill toward others with the expectation that the chain of generosity continues. Paying it forward is the natural conclusion of a team's common purpose. It's important to frame the context of what was learned, and the impact it had, sowing the seeds for future collaboration and assistance. The real goal of the Crucible is that all participants go back to their day-to-day lives ready to act as a reliable resource when called upon for insights, helping people around them grow and develop.

Think how dramatically work has changed, first with the dawn of the digital age, and then in the aftermath of a global pandemic. Yet work is still about achieving results. Though often confused with trading time for money, work is so much more. As leaders, many of us truly see our work as purposeful. We take the time to consider how the end result of what we do affects others and, in some incremental way, meaningfully improves their lives.

How we each prioritize what's most important may continue to change, but each of us has a responsibility to continuously find significant purpose and meaning in what we do. When that work has meaning, where we're free to figure out the "how" and where we're able to learn and grow, we will continue to motivate ourselves and others. Whether our job is opening doors, serving food, giving legal counsel, or leading a team of professionals in an office setting, each of us needs to think about how our work provides value to someone who benefits from our toil. And it's a responsibility of those of us who lead others to help people find real purpose and meaning in *their* work.

We can debate whether we're giving or getting enough autonomy via a hybrid work model. And we can debate whether our company's culture helps us develop expertise in certain areas. But none of us, individually or collectively, will ever truly be fulfilled if we don't derive meaning in work that serves other human beings. When we pay it forward, passing on our wisdom and success to others, when we can contribute more than we receive, we have the best chance of being truly fulfilled. To that end, paying it forward should act as a catalyst for people to recast themselves from being self-oriented to being other-oriented.

## YOUR OBLIGATION TO PAY IT FORWARD

For leaders, paying it forward is a selfless and empathetic obligation that stems from gratitude for what they've achieved and the hard-earned wisdom they have attained during their journey. Like so much of becoming a disciplined leader, paying it forward is a responsibility to bring what you've been given, earned, and learned to bear on the people you lead, the organization you're a part of, and your community at large. There are a number of ways you can exemplify paying it forward, and they start with what Socrates taught us long ago, and was discussed in the previous chapter: *know thyself.* Knowing yourself leads to self-improvement, and self-improvement allows you to fulfill your duty of serving others.

### Hone Your Leadership Edge

During a crucible of any kind, struggle, duress, and pressure bring out your true character in a way that highlights your leadership abilities—and limitations. One main takeaway from such an experience is to deepen your self-knowledge. But if you don't take the time to pause and reflect on your abilities and limitations, and just go back to merely plowing through your day-to-day responsibilities, you're missing the point. That reflection on the experience is what leads to the development of a leadership edge, one that you can pass along by role modeling the confidence, collaboration, and composure you've gained in the process of your own crucible.

One way to role model these attributes is by letting go of some control and giving people appropriate responsibilities. Your self-confidence will help others discover and gain confidence with new leadership skills while also freeing you up to build new skills that elevate your own leadership and presence. Leading with a balance of discipline and adaptability to create an inspired common purpose focuses your team on collaborative performance. Encouraging collaboration and teamwork creates a sense of community and shared purpose.

Finally, when you lead by example, you deliberately demonstrate the behaviors you want your team members to emulate. To test the example you are setting, look at your calendar. Where are you spending time? Where are you wasting time? A key lesson Crucible participants come away with is they don't need to be (and shouldn't be) busy all the time. Most of us often forget that we are not, in fact, paid to be busy. We are paid to produce results. We must produce more value than we cost. A leader's addiction to being busy is a sign of fear and a lack of trust in others. It can also be an indication they are not effectively delegating, or holding onto the work they were doing at a lower level because it is comfortable. Further, it shows a lack of self-discipline to focus on what only they can do that provides the best return on time, energy, and ultimately dollars for the organization at large. People want to follow leaders who are calm and controlled—not one who is frenetic and unfocused.

After a Crucible, one participant realized the need to slow down and focus on her people, not on "being busy." It's now routine for her to say no to most meetings so she can spend upwards of 50 percent of her time focused on developing her people. Almost every day she comes into her office, sets her backpack down, grabs a cup of coffee, and then walks around. She wasn't like that before. She explains: "I am more 'people first' focused, listening to hear if people have the direction they need and how I can help."

You must be intentional in making the time for reflection and rethinking current approaches to create a positive impact on your team, organization, and community. Fulfilling your obligations in turn will inspire others to pay it forward.

### *Mentor and Coach Others*

The most powerful way we learn is through firsthand experience. The second most powerful way is to learn from people who already *have* that firsthand experience. What you've learned through the hardships you've endured should be passed on to others, giving a better understanding of their own struggles and how to overcome them.

When you invest in others through coaching and mentoring, sharing your true self, you are inextricably linking your life with theirs. Asking thoughtful questions is key for these relationships to help your protégés identify lessons from your challenges, setbacks, and failures. Sharing those experiences can be powerful aids in helping them amplify what they have already learned, and open up ways of thinking and being to which they have not yet considered.

As an example, we ask all veteran participants of the Crucible to share their experiences of their trek and the lessons they learned about transition. This is done via social media and a videoconference, in-person, or webinar session, giving readers and listeners an opportunity to gain new understanding from them. The process of putting the experience in words, of capturing and communicating the right stories in ways that connect, helps these participants cement the lessons they will draw on in the future to continuously improve.

## THE BENEFITS OF BEING A FORCE MULTIPLIER

When you effectively pay it forward, you become a force multiplier. In essence, force multiplying develops and produces frontline leaders you can count on. To intentionally grow leaders, start by identifying leaders with potential. It's important to make the distinction between a high performer, someone who performs well in their current role, and a high potential, someone who demonstrates the ability and desire to take on more responsibility at a higher, more challenging, level. The mistake we often make when deciding who to grow into more senior roles is conflating performance with potential.

Stephen Drotter, lead author of *The Leadership Pipeline: How to Build the Leadership Powered Company*, was one of the early practitioners at GE who helped develop and apply a world-class succession process. One of the striking questions Drotter asks in his book is whether the criteria for picking leaders in your organization are actually fair. That is, free of biases like the halo effect, which is the tendency to assign positive qualities to someone based on personal preferences, such as someone who shares the same background as you. He advises leaders to distinguish between performance and potential with two criteria that indicate potential: influence among peers and the curiosity to ask questions about the bigger, more strategic picture.

Take note of whether potential leaders on your team or in your organization already possess a certain amount of clout with others, specifically peers, and are able to successfully navigate hierarchies and bureaucracies inherent in most organizations. This is an indicator that they have the ability and desire to lead with increasing levels of responsibility. Also, observe whether people ask questions at a higher level than their role, an indication they are thinking beyond the day's task as they seek to understand how their work fits into the bigger picture. These are typically the potential leaders who are not only productive, but constantly working to help the team become more efficient because they are committed to the organization. Just as you invest in these high potential leaders, they are best positioned to continue force multiplying by investing in others.

There are three specific qualities to keep in mind to become a force multiplier on your way to creating more leaders. Though these have been touched on elsewhere in the book, here they serve to not only improve your effectiveness, but to improve the efficiency of the team around you:

- **Drive.** You must be passionate and determined, thereby inspiring your team to derive purpose and meaning in their work. You must constantly push to increase your level of competency through delegating responsibility for where your team can take ownership. Your demonstrated drive will aid the team in owning outcomes, making decisions, and learning from mistakes.
- **Curiosity.** You have to be inquisitive, humble, and open to feedback so you can learn from others and continuously improve. A

culture of learning is the prerequisite for creativity, innovation, and continuous improvement—especially when faced with adversity.

- **Discipline.** You are focused on the goals and priorities with regard to the big picture and are able to persist in the face of challenges. Discipline is the key to focus and the key to persist despite external and internal setbacks. Discipline is also required to provide regular feedback, both positive and constructive, to help teammates improve their skills and grow as leaders.

Force multiplying is deliberately aimed at creating more leaders. With that in mind, strategic planning and succession planning should not be annual activities, nor should they be separate initiatives. Effective leaders routinely navigate their perspective and adeptly adjust their focus from high level to extremely tactical. They move between strategic thinking and pragmatic execution on a daily basis. When you grow your people, you grow the organization and achieve your goals. As a force multiplier, you can create a culture of learning that inspires the people you work with to become leaders themselves and create a legacy of leadership for the future. You may never fully realize the impact of investing in the high potential leaders you help because of paying it forward's ripple effect. Sometimes, you will find out what those you've helped have accomplished, or you get that little thank-you note years down the road. That feedback is worth more than all the bonuses you will ever receive—combined.

Over the course of the years, a number of Crucible participants have gone on to create their own unique experiences for others to further develop their leadership acumen. One created similar wilderness expeditions that push people to their limit. Others started nonprofit organizations to help veterans transition to civilian life. Others were inspired to produce podcasts that amplify the voices of people doing remarkable work in developing leaders. All of them have paid it forward in a way that has created a lasting effect on the world around them, and their efforts continue to inspire us in our work as well.

**PRO TIP**

Storytelling is one of the most powerful tools leaders have in their toolboxes, and it is the one they most often neglect. Our ability to tell engaging stories is a leader differentiator. When told well, stories illuminate the lessons we want our audience to learn and allow the listener to emotionally connect with us. An effective story is remembered far longer than direction, facts, figures, and financial goals. When you think of your own hard-earned lessons, what is the story you tell that emboldens and helps others the most? We encourage you to rehearse the story that delivers the lessons you want to convey to make it truly impactful. Practice in the mirror, and to actual audiences (start small and with those you trust) who will give you feedback and help you shape your narrative in such a way that it packs the intended punch.

▲▲▲

Now take a moment to consider your own organization and how you approach paying it forward:

- What is your practice for reflecting and capturing stories that demonstrate paying it forward?
- How do you help others develop more curiosity to make better decisions?
- Looking at your calendar over the past two to four weeks, are you investing in people and projects that reflect what you truly value?

## THE REST OF THE STORY

By putting his lessons on a whiteboard, in a visible place for others to see, Robert, the Fortune 500 executive mentioned at the beginning of this chapter, was able to stimulate conversations with his team about the lessons he learned on his expedition and the skills and behaviors he was working to improve. When people asked him for clarity on items such as "be kind," he was able to pass on his stories from the Crucible to bring the lessons to life, while also highlighting how not being kind could have far-reaching and long-term adverse effects.

It was impossible for his teammates to not talk with him about the insights on his whiteboard and to not notice the commitment he made, and kept, for continuous improvement. His transparency invited his team to both reflect on their own experiences while also gaining valuable insights from him. It is not an overstatement to say his team became far more compassionate, resilient, productive, and effective after their leader's Crucible experience.

## CONCLUSION

Henri Frédéric Amiel, a nineteenth-century Swiss philosopher, wrote, "Our duty is to be useful, not according to our desires but according to our powers." On many occasions, Crucible participants discuss what they want to do versus what they should do, and we question how they will use their gifts to serve others and pay it forward. Participants are asked to consider whether their goals are truly aspirational enough, and if sacrifices for the benefit of others will make them more fulfilled than being focused on their own comfort, pleasure, and personal achievement. When personal fulfillment is a goal, the natural focus is almost always on serving others, paying it forward, and setting aside other, more common definitions of success. By embodying the philosophy of paying it forward, you can create a positive and contagious ripple effect that inspires and encourages others to do the same. Paying it forward can also help create a culture of mutual support, respect, and growth.

## THE THREE PILLARS

### *Leading Self*

It is possible to go through a crucible experience and learn little if you don't take the time to slow down, reflect, and seek feedback.

- What did you learn from your last crucible experience, and how did you share those lessons with others?
- Who can you ask to capture deeper insights from your struggles?
- When you compare your life with the one you envision, what are the most significant changes that will have to occur in order to accomplish your goals?

### *Leading Others*

The significance of leadership is that we are entrusted with the responsibility to grow and develop others into leaders themselves. It's the leader's responsibility to create a sense of duty for long-lasting inclusion, belonging, and true engagement.

- Who on your team could benefit from one or more of the lessons you've learned through your crucible experiences?
- How can you leverage your own learning to more effectively coach your teammates through their crucibles?
- In what ways can you empower your teammates during times of challenge to support the team and organization?

### *Leading the Organization*

Just as people go through crucibles, so do organizations. Learning organizations not only survive these hard times, but can thrive and come out stronger on the other side.

- Reflecting on the last challenge your organization endured, what lessons were learned and how are they being used for continuous improvement?
- What might prevent your organization from achieving its vision?
- How can you leverage your high potential leaders to help uncover the root causes of problems and issues to create opportunities for growth?

# CONCLUSION

> "I realized that I don't want an easy life. I felt most at home in the dirt, without a shower, carrying heavy stuff on my back with people I liked. I reclaimed who I am and how I want to feel—empowered, competent, capable, and powerful."
>
> —*Courtney Wilson, Veteran Participant, Moab Crucible*

On a glacier in Patagonia, we planted a seed with the participants. We inferred that the expected outcome of the expedition would be how to accelerate the development of a high performing team. During the trek, an executive participant stopped the group in the middle of an ascent. The team worried that something was wrong. Had he hurt himself? Did he notice a crevasse up ahead? What was happening? It turned out, everything was going just fine. He had just had an *aha* moment.

Looking around at each member of the group, he said, "You know how we're trying to figure out how to accelerate the development of a high performance team?" We all nodded, listening intently, the wind whipping our faces, the sun glaring in our eyes. He added, "What if team development has a terminal velocity? Remember from physics . . . 'Terminal velocity is the final and fastest speed achieved by an object falling through the air.' Like a skydiver who feels the sense of falling until they hit about 126 miles per hour and then they feel like they are floating. If the most important components of a high performing team are trust and a shared purpose, maybe we can only go as fast as humans can grow to trust each other through experiences that test selflessness and reliability." He was on to something. How people are tested, and what they glean from those experiences, causes them to question their assumptions. And when assumptions can be removed, egos put aside, and vulnerability embraced, true trust blooms.

The future of leadership lies in cultivating a shared trust, one that is palpable and steadfast. As a leader, you must grant others agency, placing trust in them and their ability to make responsible decisions, because when you give trust, you earn trust in return. Embracing the crucible-like journey of leadership, and adopting a personalized approach centered on trust and empowerment, allows you to navigate complexities, effectively serving those you lead to contribute to noble pursuits and a successful future. Your narrative changes as you help others change theirs.

One topic that seems to come up a lot during a Crucible is the desire to define a good life. Following that introspection and the Crucible experience, we've seen many people make major pivots in their lives to do work according to what they hold dear. We've seen longtime corporate types become successful entrepreneurs. We've seen people make healthier lifestyle choices, and some even set adventurous goals to climb mountains with their kids. Some used the experience to process hard lessons they learned transitioning from the military to civilian life. Some processed failure, firings, and relationship breakups. Some took the lessons back to their organizational teams with a certain vulnerability and experienced rapid growth in their ability to lead and influence others.

We've seen people develop more self-awareness, and for the first time, really reflect on how their behavior affects others. They have then used that knowledge to resolve to deliver deliberate responses for the good of others, even if it meant putting their pride and ego in the back seat. Finally, we've seen people trained in psychology attend Crucibles, and though their input helped us validate our curriculum, we believe we helped them be even more effective in their work, influencing people to become healthier in emotional, mental, physical, and even spiritual aspects of their lives.

As a twenty-first-century leader, it's time to embrace a new leadership paradigm that emphasizes what it means to be self-reliant. You must know when to lead and when to follow, recognize and develop your strengths and those of your team members, and foster your growth and the realization of your aspirations. Achieving this personalized leadership approach requires reflection, letting go of strengths that no longer serve you, and persistently addressing shortcomings to forge ahead.

The powerful, challenging experiences encountered in all phases of a crucible, whether in the wilderness or in daily life, reinforce learning and foster the exchange of new ways to solve difficult problems. The special aspect of the Crucible is that it is done alongside extraordinary peers with similar drive and interests. We make a singular guarantee that our participants will not be the same leaders they were after the Crucible as they were before. Can you make that guarantee for the people you lead?

Indomitable organizations begin and end with people who are presented with, and accept, opportunities for growth and development. And people only grow when their personal drivers align with the values, vision, and goals of the organization. The environment must also be one of positivity, where there is a mindset of abundance, not one of scarcity, an environment that fosters disciplined duty and grit in all pursuits, providing the glue that keeps a team focused even when the going gets tough. By creating an environment where both grit and disciplined duty are valued, expected, and reinforced, your team will become indomitable.

When we apply the takeaways after the expeditions have concluded, the lessons come to life as a comprehensive leadership approach for the real world, with real teams, facing real problems. The crucible metaphor aptly captures the transformative power of adversity in shaping individuals into indomitable teams. Through crucible experiences of any sort, people gain profound insights, revelations, and lessons that enable them to understand the intrinsic power of discipline, grit, and positivity.

This book is not a checklist, but a framework for becoming a self-reliant leader in service to building an indomitable team. Our aim has been to provide insights that help improve your leadership effectiveness to create a lasting, rippling impact on the teams you lead today and in the future. We want to inspire you to leverage the inevitable crucibles you will face so you can become mentally stronger, more aware, and reach your highest potential for the benefit of those you lead.

Now it's your turn to put what you have learned here into practice. Listed below are key topics we've outlined throughout the book. Read each one carefully, and pick only one of the twelve listed below to focus on today. When you know you've made progress in that one area, revisit the list below, and choose the next area of focus for your development. Share what you're working on with mentors, and invite your teammates into the conversation for advice and suggestions.

1. **Selection: Selecting the Right People vs. Best People.** Selection is an ongoing process by which standards are upheld, and culture is not just a word, but something people internalize to accomplish heroic aspirations. Ensure selection is based on behaviors that align with what is truly valued.
2. **Preparation: Getting Squared Away.** Help people discover real purpose and meaning in their role. In doing so, you create that elusive sense of duty—a shared accountability that separates excellent teams from uncommon, extraordinary, and high performing teams.

3. **First Encounter: Being Authentic and Vulnerable.** Team members are expected to be authentic and vulnerable, and everyone must treat each other with dignity and respect, while holding their views lightly. You have to care to listen. You have to listen to hear. You have to hear to feel. And you have to feel to lead.
4. **Movement: Setting Direction, Pace, and Tone.** Self-reliant leaders take the time to effectively define, communicate, and model the pace they expect of their teammates and consider the impact on teams and families. You must create a sustainable environment where people feel valued, and have a gratitude of privilege that they are part of something big, important, and noble.
5. **Base Camp: Reenergizing and Reengaging.** Base camp isn't the finish line—it's another starting point. It's a deliberate and well-planned rest. Acknowledge and appreciate the effort and progress in the moment.
6. **Fireside Chat: Accelerating Relationships.** A fireside chat is an opportunity to elicit a diverse range of perspectives that are shared and heard. They can then be incorporated into improving trust, gaining commitment, and enhancing the organization's culture through unassailable bonds of social capital.
7. **Who's Who? Cultivating the Group Dynamic.** Create an environment where purpose is clear and shared accountability is seen as a sacred duty. Letting other people down when it comes to commitments, promises, and obligations is simply not an option.
8. **Obstacles: Expecting Adversity.** Adversity can also be a tool for exponential learning and growth, as well as a bonding experience that can strengthen the team. Buried in the setbacks and hard times are the seeds of future victories if you take the time to step back, reset, refocus, and reenergize your team.

9. **Rhythm: Creating Synergy.** The strong, regular, repeated pattern of movement leads to a collective state of flow in which progress for the organization becomes inevitable. Creating and maintaining that rhythm demands a combination of vision, discipline, effectiveness, and adaptability, all with an ingrained sense of duty at the core.
10. **Tribal Connections: Cementing Commitments.** Crucibles create an opportunity to forge fast and profound friendships, distinguished by remarkably strong bonds. It's in those bonds—those deep and meaningful human connections—where dreams are shared, aspirations expanded, and commitments formed.
11. **The Crux: Bringing It All Together.** Amidst all the challenges you face, you can maintain a fierce optimism when grounded in the "why" of your work. When there's alignment, you develop a sense of duty to those you work with, and you're able to demonstrate persistence and determination in the face of the biggest challenges. It's those deeds that role model what you wish to see in others, and it's the crux of what you do as a self-reliant leader.
12. **The End Is Another Beginning: Paying It Forward.** By embodying the philosophy of paying it forward, you create a positive and contagious ripple effect that inspires and encourages others to do the same. Paying it forward can also help create a culture of mutual support, respect, and growth.

We hope we've imparted you with lessons, ideas, and motivation to help you become the best leader you can be. And though we can't recommend a wilderness expedition enough to help you realize your leadership goals, we recognize not every business leader will undertake such a journey. And in many ways, you don't have to.

All of us are tested and tried in some way every day, whether it be at work, at school, at home, or anywhere in between. As a whole, we have a never-ending supply of trials and tribulations. Despite being more connected than ever before, we need to find ways to communicate more effectively. Whether an international pandemic, economic recessions, or political and social upheaval, it's the challenge of our time to morph, adapt, and grow in ways that serve our teams, organizations, institutions, and society at large.

What really matters, though, is how we come out of our own personal crucibles that often change our narrative. How we uncover the true leaders we can be through determination and dedication, integrity and trust. Honing our virtues takes time and patience, which is why you need to slow down to speed up. We invite you to do just that. Take a step back, filter out the noise, and take the time to develop yourself and your team. Get into situations outside of your comfort zone. Get out into nature and feel the awe it can inspire. Find your crucible and find yourself.

# CRUCIBLE TESTIMONIALS

"There are a lot of ways to develop the next generation of high potential leaders, but the Self-Reliant Leadership Crucible® is 100 percent proven. Your leaders will be forever changed to the benefit of their teams and your entire organization."

*—Rear Admiral Kerry Metz, Retired U.S. Navy SEAL*

"I recently returned from spending four amazing days on a life-changing expedition with a bunch of Green Berets in the extreme backcountry of Moab, Utah. The Crucible brings together corporate leaders and military veterans transitioning to the civilian workforce. The idea is that whether your background is in business or the military, you will come away having gained valuable new perspectives, including insight into how we 'show up' as leaders under circumstances of extreme adversity. Western Union (WU) has been a key sponsor of the program over the last couple of years because we support veteran hiring, and value the integrity, leadership, and teamwork skills veterans bring to the table."

*—Jacqueline Molnar, Chief Compliance Officer, Western Union*

"Jan Rutherford and his team pair transitioning military members to senior business leaders in an open environment, helping them realize they already possess the skills necessary to tackle today's business challenges: leadership, teamwork, critical problem-solving skills, resourcefulness, resilience, and a high adversity quotient. I couldn't have asked for a better opportunity to help me understand how my last year at Amazon and my previous eight in the Coast Guard related to one another and what improvements could be made in my ability to help lead and be a part of successful teams in the future."

*—Maggie Ward, Program Manager, Amazon, Coast Guard Veteran*

"I joined one of the Crucible Expeditions to support veterans' transition into the civilian sector, and I was totally blown away. It was intimate, painful, and empowering. Jan organized, planned, and executed an experience that will forever change my life. He surrounds himself with amazing people with whom you want to connect."

*—Kimberly Jung, Co-founder, Rumi Spice, Army Veteran*

"One of the cornerstones of success for this mission execution was the constant teamwork from our group that seemed to grow immediately after we met, through all the daily challenges, until the end of the Crucible. The bond between this team crystallized through our in-depth discussions centering on what the key ingredients are to a successful team. We walked out of that desert in Moab armed with new tools and new knowledge that will enrich our respective teams and, as an extension of that, enrich the organizations to which we belong."

*—Bridget Abraham, Executive at Western Union*

"Attending a Crucible Expedition is, hands down, the best leadership experience I have ever completed. The expeditions are some of the most rewarding experiences on so many levels. I am forever enriched by the new friends I've gained through this profoundly unique experience."

*—Jim Vaselopulos, Founder & CEO of Rafti Advisors*

"The Crucible reminds us of what it was that made us successful, but does so in a much more powerful way . . . by removing the comfort of the familiar. The Self-Reliant Leadership Crucible helps us find the courage to step away from the familiar and lead people to achieve extraordinary ends that we would otherwise not realize through simply continuing down the path that we have always known."

*—Mike Petschel, Country Manager,*
*Molson Coors, Army Veteran*

"At first, I thought they were just being humble when they said, 'It is all about the other people on this trip—they are the ones you will learn from.' However, I soon saw that the weekend was less a traditional leadership seminar and more a carefully guided team experience, one ultimately defined by our own actions. The conversations shared along the trail, while making dinner, or during breaks were rich in content and genuine in nature. Everyone on this trip wanted to share—and most importantly—they wanted to learn."

*—Michael Meehan, Business Analyst,*
*Perpetual Motion, Army Veteran*

# NOTES


## INTRODUCTION

1. "State of the Global Workplace 2023 Report: The Voice of the World's Employees," Gallup, accessed June 28, 2023, https://www.gallup.com/workplace/349484/state-of-the-global-workplace.aspx.
2. Melissa Angell, "There's No Slowing the Great Resignation," *Inc.*, January 6, 2022, https://www.inc.com/melissa-angell/great-resignation-hits-new-record-november-jobs.html.

## CHAPTER 1

1. Frederick Herzberg, "One More Time: How Do You Motivate Employees?," hbr.org, *Harvard Business Review*, January 2003, https://hbr.org/2003/01/one-more-time-how-do-you-motivate-employee.
2. Jan Rutherford and Jim Vaselopulos, "161: We Don't Hire People to Fulfill a Function, We Hire People to Fulfill a Purpose," July 31, 2019, *The Leadership Podcast*, podcast, MP3 audio, 41:35, https://theleadershippodcast.com/tlp161-we-dont-hire-people-to-fulfill-a-function-we-hire-people-to-fulfill-a-purpose-horst-schulze/.
3. Bradford D. Smart, *Topgrading, 3rd Edition: The Proven Hiring and Promoting Method that Turbocharges Company Performance* (New York, NY: Portfolio, 2012).

## CHAPTER 2

1. Joe Allen, "'One Bad Meeting Causes Three More Meetings': Companies Are Fighting Back Against Meeting Bloat," financialpost.com, Financial Post, February 18, 2022, https://financialpost.com/fp-work

/one-bad-meeting-causes-three-more-meetings-companies-are-fighting-back-against-meeting-bloat.

## CHAPTER 3

1. Jack Zenger and Joseph Folkman, "The Ideal Praise-to-Criticism Ratio," hbr.org, *Harvard Business Review*, March 15, 2013, https://hbr.org/2013/03/the-ideal-praise-to-criticism?autocomplete=true.

## CHAPTER 4

1. Alok Patel and Stephanie Plowman, "The Increasing Importance of a Best Friend at Work," Gallup, August 17, 2022, https://www.gallup.com/workplace/397058/increasing-importance-best-friend-work.aspx.
2. Quoteresearch, "Plans Are Worthless, but Planning Is Everything," Quote Investigator, updated October 28, 2021, https://quoteinvestigator.com/2017/11/18/planning/.
3. W. Chan Kim and Renée Mauborgne, "Parables of Leadership," hbr.org, *Harvard Business Review*, July–August 1992, https://hbr.org/1992/07/parables-of-leadership.

## CHAPTER 5

1. D. S. Yeager, V. Purdie-Vaughns, J. Garcia, N. Apfel, P. Brzustoski, A. Master, W. Hessert, M. Williams, and G. L. Cohen, "Breaking the Cycle of Mistrust: Wise Interventions to Provide Critical Feedback Across the Racial Divide," *Journal of Experimental Psychology: General*, 143 (2014): 809.
2. Kim Cameron, *Positively Energizing Leadership: Virtuous Actions and Relationships That Create High Performance* (Oakland, CA: Berrett-Koehler Publishers, 2021), 3.

## CHAPTER 6

1. Jan Rutherford and Jim Vaselopulos, "81: If You're Talking About Trust, It Probably Doesn't Exist," January 24, 2018, *The Leadership Podcast*, podcast, MP3 audio, 36:05, https://theleadershippodcast.com/tlp081-if-youre-talking-about-trust-it-probably-doesnt-exist/?doing_wp_cron=1681149675.6484539508819580078125.

## CHAPTER 7


1. Ron Friedman, "5 Things High Performing Teams Do Differently," hbr.org, *Harvard Business Review*, October 21, 2021, https://hbr.org/2021/10/5-things-high-performing-teams-do-differently.
2. Bruce W. Tuckman and Mary A. Jensen, "Stages of Small-Group Development Revisited," *Group & Organization Management*, 2(4) (1977): 420.
3. "Be Bold: The Story of Billie Jean King vs Bobby Riggs," homage.com, March 29, 2022, https://www.homage.com/blogs/news/be-bold-the-story-of-billie-jean-king-vs-bobby-riggs.


## CHAPTER 8


1. Nate Bennett and G. James Lemoine, "What VUCA Really Means for You," hbr.org, *Harvard Business Review*, January–February 2014, https://hbr.org/2014/01/what-vuca-really-means-for-you.
2. Carol S. Dweck, *Mindset: The New Psychology of Success* (New York: Random House, 2006), 21.
3. Dweck, *Mindset*, 15.
4. Susan Ratcliffe, ed., *Oxford Essential Quotations*, Oxford Reference, Oxford University Press, 2016, https://www.oxfordreference.com/display/10.1093/acref/9780191826719.001.0001/q-oro-ed4-00003260;jsessionid=5BCD3009E6EFCDA929D2B9C0EAEB47CF.
5. Drake Baer, "How Your 'Locus of Control' Drives Your Success (and Stress)," *Business Insider*, July 30, 2014, https://www.businessinsider.com/proactive-people-are-successful-and-less-stressed-2014-7.


## CHAPTER 9


1. "About LinkedIn," LinkedIn, accessed June 28, 2023, https://about.linkedin.com/.
2. Harish Dash, "Crafting a Clear and Compelling Vision and Mission: Why Everyone Needs One," March 3, 2023, https://www.linkedin.com/pulse/crafting-clear-compelling-vision-mission-why-everyone-harish-dash/.
3. "Patagonia's Mission Statement," Patagonia, accessed June 28, 2023, https://www.patagonia.com.hk/pages/our-mission.
4. "About LinkedIn."
5. "About Google," Google, accessed June 28, 2023, https://about.google/.
6. Will Gardner, "Patagonia: Mission & Values," willgardner.co, January 30, 2018, https://willgardner.co/patagonia-mission-values/.

7. "New Surgeon General Advisory Raises Alarm About the Devastating Impact of the Epidemic of Loneliness and Isolation in America," hhs.gov, U.S. Department of Health and Human Services, May 3, 2023, https://www.hhs.gov/about/news/2023/05/03/new-surgeon-general-advisory-raises-alarm-about-devastating-impact-epidemic-loneliness-isolation-united-states.html.

## CHAPTER 10

1. Alok Patel and Stephanie Plowman, "The Increasing Importance of a Best Friend at Work," Gallup, August 17, 2022, https://www.gallup.com/workplace/397058/increasing-importance-best-friend-work.aspx.
2. Jan Rutherford and Jim Vaselopulos, "199: A Just Cause with Simon Sinek," April 29, 2020, *The Leadership Podcast*, podcast, MP3 audio, 44:47, https://theleadershippodcast.com/tlp199-a-just-cause-with-simon-sinek/.
3. Jan Rutherford and Jim Vaselopulos, "121: Jeffrey Pfeffer Challenges Our Assumptions About Leadership," October 24, 2018, *The Leadership Podcast*, podcast, MP3 audio, 46:47, https://theleadershippodcast.com/tlp-121-jeffrey-pfeffer-challenges-our-assumptions-about-leadership/.
4. Morgan Smith, "40% of Workers Are Considering Quitting Their Jobs Soon—Here's Where They're Going," cnbc.com, Make It, updated July 21, 2022, https://www.cnbc.com/2022/07/20/40percent-of-workers-are-considering-quitting-their-jobs-soon.html.
5. Jan Rutherford, "Self-Reliant Leadership Courses," Self-Reliant Leadership, accessed June 28, 2023, https://selfreliantleadership.teachable.com.

## CHAPTER 11

1. Rohan Rajiv, "Good Tired and Bad Tired—Harry Chapin," *A Learning a Day* (blog), September 18, 2015, https://alearningaday.blog/2015/09/28/good-tired-and-bad-tired-harry-chapin/.
2. Jan Rutherford and Jim Vaselopulos, "101: General Stanley McChrystal on What Connects Us," June 6, 2018, *The Leadership Podcast*, podcast, MP3 audio, 48:05, https://theleadershippodcast.com/tlp101-general-stanley-mcchrystal-on-what-connects-us/.

# ACKNOWLEDGMENTS

We would like to thank all of the alumni who have participated in Self-Reliant Leadership Crucible Expeditions over the years, and especially those who contributed their stories and lessons learned for this book. You have made this journey come to life, and we thank you for paying it forward and allowing others to learn from the wisdom gained from your experience.

Vik Bakshi
Christen Beck
Terence Bennett
Brad Billingsley
JR Bond
Matt Breidenbach
Tim Cole
Jeff Engelstad
Jason Field
Kevin Glynn
Jim Hogan
Dan Kanefsky
Julie Keller
Kyle Kennedy
Brian Kollmeyer
Rodney Macon
Taylor Manson
Will Markham
Dan Marostica
Mike Merzke
Jacqueline Molnar
Father Daniel Nolan
Jay Packard
Al Paxton
Jim Peters
Mike Petschel
Shani Phillips
Erin Procko
Alex Racey
Alberto Ramos
Nikki Rizzi
Lou Rosen
Dave Scott
Steven Scott
Adam Steelhammer
Wade Stencel
Sheryl Tullis
Meg Vanderlaan
Jim Vaselopulos
Waldo Waldman
Evan Williams
Courtney Wilson

It takes a village, as they say, and, for us, it all started with Susan Williams, Senior Content Manager at LinkedIn. With vim and vigor, and all the positivity and more encouragement than authors should expect, she made all sorts of generous introductions, and of those, two were critical. Todd Sattersten helped with the early concept of the book and asked all the right questions authors should be asked before they take on a big project. His acumen of the publishing world is without peer. Susan then introduced us to Jeff Leeson, another notably connected professional in the publishing world.

To our great fortune, Jeff introduced us to the talented Zach Gajewski, editor-extraordinaire. Zach was always positive, encouraging, yet never offered praise that wasn't warranted. He was honest in his counsel, and always respectful and dignified. We can't say we always enjoyed getting his redlines back (truly nothing is more humbling than writing a book with an editor of his caliber), but this book is infinitely better because of our partnership with Zach. He didn't just get our manuscript after we wrote the first draft—he worked with us hand in hand over the course of nearly two years to bring this book to life. He not only improved our writing, but his approach typified the traits of leaders we wrote about in this book. What a gift he's been, and with heartfelt thanks, we want to acknowledge his outsized contribution to bringing this book to you.

Zach introduced us to John Willig, a book agent who possessed an upbeat and inquisitive approach, and untold wisdom from his vast experience in the publishing world. We don't know how long the average agent takes to get a publishing deal, but in retrospect, it seemed like we met John one week, and had a contract the next. Thank you, John.

The book deal John secured was with Matt Holt and his extraordinary team at BenBella. When we were networking with all the people Susan Williams introduced us to, there were just five publishers we kept hearing about where our book would be a great fit. BenBella was at the top of the list with everyone, and we feel very fortunate to have Matt's team behind this book. Whether it was iterating on cover design, pressure testing our content, or educating us on the intricacies of publication that were entirely foreign to us, the Matt Holt team made us feel comfortable and optimistic for the continued journey. Any author would be fortunate to work with this great team.

We'd also like to thank General Stanley McChrystal for the brilliant foreword. Stan has been gracious with interviews over the years, and didn't hesitate for a minute to introduce this book to our readers. He's one of the best examples out there of a veteran successfully transitioning to civilian life, and paying it forward as a true force multiplier. And we thank Ellen Chapin for her assistance in getting the foreword done in record time. A super talented writer in her own right—and someone whose career trajectory we'll be tracking.

## FROM JAN RUTHERFORD . . .

The very first Crucible came together thanks to my partnership with Brad Billingsley. And it was Brad who introduced me to Vince Anderson, the world-class alpinist from Skyward Mountaineering. Vince and his team have been our guides on nearly all the Crucibles to date—most notably the expedition to Patagonia. Also, the guide with the most experience on our trips has been Steven VanSickle, and his patience and humor have always been in balance at the right time in the right place. The biggest accolades we can give Skyward is that they have kept our teams safe, which is always our top priority.

Other big supporters over the years have been Steve House, Jacqueline Molnar, Sean Conley, and *The Leadership Podcast* co-host, Jim Vaselopulos, who has participated in big ways on three of the Crucibles—Moab, Patagonia, and western Colorado. Also, a big shout-out to all the videographers we've had on the Crucibles over the years. No one works harder on those trips than the man or woman carrying the heaviest pack—and running all over the place to get the most incredible shots.

Every day since I created Self-Reliant Leadership, I have channeled two of the most important mentors of my professional life—Jim Downey and the late Bud Ahearn. I wouldn't be where I am without the question they asked me often rattling around in my brain: "What's a good life—and are you living one?"

I wanted to write this book with a colleague, someone I liked, trusted, and respected. Ideally, that person would be a Crucible alumnus, a military veteran who attended and taught at one of the most prestigious institutions of higher learning in our country, and was of a different generation and gender . . . Wouldn't you know, that perfect collaborator and co-author was actually out there, and even better, she agreed to co-author this book. Thank you, Jacquie Jordan.

Thanks to my parents, who instilled in me a disciplined work ethic, and for always keeping me humble.

I have always appreciated my son's perspective, especially his curiosity about what makes for successful transitions. His questions have helped me continually refine the curriculum of the Crucible, and the overall approach to my work.

My daughter worked with me during the critical growth phase of my business, and her counsel, based on her keen insight of people and problems, was always the right advice I needed at the right time. I wouldn't have made some of the tough decisions along the way without her advice.

My wife is a saint. Truly. Patient, wise, encouraging, truthful, and beyond selfless. You don't take on a book project without sacrificing family time, and there has never been anything but unwavering support. I don't know what I ever did to deserve her, but I sure am grateful every single day for her love and support.

## FROM JACQUIE JORDAN . . .

From the moment I met Jan, on a phone interview hoping to join a Crucible, completely uncertain of what my future looked like, he's always invested in me. That means he sometimes tells me things I don't know about myself or don't want to admit. I was honored that he believed in me enough, even knowing my flaws, to ask me to collaborate with him on this project so we could continue to invest in others. I think we're both better for the connection. I know I am.

I was only in a position to be considered as a Crucible participant with heroic aspirations thanks to a number of mentors, leaders, and friends who have poured into me along my journey. The names are too many to recount in this space, but I hope I have conveyed to each of you over the years what you have meant in my growth and development, both professionally and personally. "Thanks!"

To my mom and sisters—thanks for helping me become a woman who has the capacity and drive to give to others. Through watching selflessness in action as you each give to and teach others, I have been, and continue to be, inspired.

It's not a stretch to say this book wouldn't be possible without my partner as he not only helped me calibrate my thinking along the way, but he introduced me to Jan to begin with. A partner who fully believes in your dreams and helps you create both a meaningful and enjoyable life along the way is priceless. Thank you, Dustin, for forever expanding my horizons and what I am capable of—what we are capable of, together.